PENGUIN BOOKS

THE WORLD OF ODYSSEUS

M. I. Finley was born in New York City in 1912. He obtained an M.A. in public law and a Ph.D. in ancient history at Columbia University. After working as research assistant in Roman law at Columbia University in 1933–4, he became editor and translator at the Institute of Social Research (then affiliated with Columbia University) and taught history at the City College of New York. He was Assistant Professor of History at Rutgers University from 1948 to 1952. In 1955 he became a lecturer in the Faculty of Classics at Cambridge University and two years later was elected a Fellow of Jesus College. He became Reader in Ancient Social and Economic History there in 1966 and was Professor of Ancient History from 1970 to 1980; he was Master of Darwin College from 1976 until 1982 when he was made Honorary Fellow. In 1971 he was elected a Fellow of the British Academy; he was knighted in 1979.

Sir Moses Finley is the author of *Studies in Land and Credit in Ancient Athens* (1952), *The Ancient Greeks* (1963), *Aspects of Antiquity* (1968, second edition 1977), *Ancient Sicily to the Arab Conquest* (1968), *Early Greece: The Bronze and Archaic Ages* (1970), *Democracy Ancient and Modern* (1973), *The Ancient Economy* (1973), *The Use and Abuse of History* (1975), *Ancient Slavery and Modern Ideology* (1980), *Economy and Society in Ancient Greece* (1981), *Politics in the Ancient World* (1983), *Ancient History: Evidence and Models* (1985), co-author (with H. W. Pleket) of *The Olympic Games: The First Thousand Years* (1976), editor of *The Portable Greek Historians: The Essence of Herodotus, Thucydides, Xenophon, Polybius* (1959), and editor of the series *Ancient Culture and Society* (since 1969). He died in 1986.

M. I. FINLEY

THE WORLD OF ODYSSEUS

*

SECOND EDITION

PENGUIN BOOKS

PENGUIN BOOKS

Published by the Penguin Group
Penguin Books Ltd, 27 Wrights Lane, London W8 5TZ, England
Penguin Books USA Inc., 375 Hudson Street, New York, New York 10014, USA
Penguin Books Australia Ltd, Ringwood, Victoria, Australia
Penguin Books Canada Ltd, 10 Alcorn Avenue, Toronto, Ontario, Canada M4V 3B2
Penguin Books (NZ) Ltd, 182–190 Wairau Road, Auckland 10, New Zealand

Penguin Books Ltd, Registered Offices: Harmondsworth, Middlesex, England

First published in the United States of America
by The Viking Press 1954
Revised Edition first published in Great Britain by Chatto & Windus 1956
Published in Pelican Books in Great Britain 1962
Reprinted with revisions 1967, 1972
Revised Edition first published in the United States of America
by Viking Compass 1965
Second Revised Edition first published in Great Britain by Chatto & Windus 1978
Second Revised Edition first published in the United States of America
by The Viking Press 1978
Published in Pelican Books in Great Britain 1979
Published in Pelican Books in the United States of America 1979
Reprinted in Penguin Books 1991
3 5 7 9 10 8 6 4 2

Printed in England by Clays Ltd, St Ives plc
Set in Baskerville

For Mary — again

CONTENTS

PREFACE

It is awkward for an author to preface the new edition of a book which has frequently been reprinted, in ten languages, since its original publication twenty-two years ago; which has been cited, discussed, attacked in innumerable books and articles, and which has been the acknowledged starting-point of studies by other historians of society and of ideas. It would be wrong to pull the text apart in order to argue the methodological issues the book has raised, rather by implication, or other controversial topics. For such matters, the reader is referred to the two Appendices which are new in this edition and to the bibliographical essay at the end.

The text itself must stand on its own and remain what it has always been, a picture of a society, based on a close reading of the *Iliad* and *Odyssey*, supported by study of other societies to help elucidate obscure points in the poems. The social institutions and values make up a coherent system, and, from our present outlook, a very alien one, but neither an improbable nor an unfamiliar one in the experience of modern anthropology. That the ancient Greeks in subsequent centuries and classicists in the nineteenth century were unable to comprehend it without resorting to allegory and symbolic 'interpretation' is irrelevant. It is equally beside the point that the narrative is a collection of fictions from beginning to end.

Homeric scholarship has become notorious for its unmanageable quantity, further multiplied by a sea of publications following Michael Ventris's decipherment of the Linear B tablets. A few experts have read more of it, Homeric and Mycenaean, than I have, regularly and systematically, in the past quarter-century, but there cannot be many. If, therefore, this new edition does not appear to be very different in long stretches, an explanation is required. I have not rewritten anything merely in the interest of stylistic improvement, or just in order to rewrite. I have corrected errors, added new information or new insights when they were known to me and seemed relevant to my account. However, I have found no cause to alter in any essentials the three substantive chapters; on the contrary, the picture I drew in those chapters has, I believe, been further confirmed by more recent scholarship. In my presidential address to the Classical Association in 1974 (Appendix I) I said that I proposed to re-examine in particular the account of the common people in Chapter 3. Even there, in the end, I found no better or alternative formulation beyond a slight change in nuance in the wording.

On one topic the confirmation has been so strong that I have felt free to make a major deletion. When I wrote the book, in the early 1950s, the notion was generally accepted that the world of Odysseus was on the whole the Mycenaean world, which came to an abrupt end, by violence, around 1200 B.C. The small heretical minority, of whom I was one, were in a difficult polemical position, and in 1956 I added an Appendix, 'A Note on Homer and the Mycenaean Tablets', which has appeared in all subsequent editions. Today it is no longer seriously maintained, though it is still said often enough, that the *Iliad* and *Odyssey* reflect Mycenaean society, a modern construct, it is important to note, which no ancient Greek had ever heard of. The decipherment of the Linear B tablets and archaeology together have destroyed the old orthodoxy. I have therefore dropped that Appendix, but I cannot resist pointing out that proper concern for social institutions and social history had anticipated what philology and archaeology subsequently found.

About oral poetry and its techniques, in contrast, the alterations (in the first two chapters) are significant, though not numerous. I originally wrote at a time when the discoveries of Milman Parry, which revolutionized our understanding of heroic poetry, had just been digested by scholars in the English-speaking world, and were still largely ignored elsewhere. Since then there has been much progress in this field, and I have revised my text accordingly. That is to say, I have followed the views I find myself most in agreement with, on a subject still torn by controversy (again I refer to the bibliographical essay) — about the relative stability or instability of the 'formulas', the structural unity of each poem, and the creative genius of the poet (or poets) responsible for the *Iliad* and *Odyssey* we possess.

I have nevertheless retained a few quotations from modern authors which are now 'out of date', though no less correct for that, as a token of renewed gratitude to writers who influenced my thinking at the start. For the same reason, I repeat the thanks to individual friends recorded in the first edition: C. M. Arensberg, Nathan Halper, Herbert Marcuse, Martin Ostwald, Friedrich Solmsen, and the late Pascal Covici and Karl Polanyi.

M.I.F.

A Note on Homeric Citations

All quotations from the two poems are by book and line number. Books of the *Iliad* are given in Roman numerals, of the *Odyssey* in Arabic numerals. It is therefore unnecessary to indicate the title of the poem on each occasion.

THRACE

Hellespont
(Dardanelles)

● Hissarlik (Ilion)

TROAD

LEMNOS

LESBOS

ASIA

AEGEAN

LYDIA

MINOR

CHIOS

SEA

SAMOS

● Colophon

● Ephesus

CARIA

Miletus ●

DELOS

● Halicarnassus

20 40 60 80 100 MILES

100 K.M.

RHODES

Chapter 1

HOMER AND THE GREEKS

'By the general consent of criticks,' wrote Dr Johnson, 'the first praise of genius is due to the writer of an epick poem, as it requires an assemblage of all the powers which are singly sufficient for other compositions.' He was thinking of John Milton then, and he concluded his life of the English poet with these words: 'His work is not the greatest of heroick poems, only because it is not the first.' That title had been pre-empted for all time by Homer, whom the Greeks called simply 'the poet'.

No other poet, no other literary figure in all history for that matter, occupied a place in the life of his people such as Homer's. He was their pre-eminent symbol of nationhood, the unimpeachable authority on their earliest history, and a decisive figure in the creation of their pantheon, as well as their most beloved and most widely quoted poet. Plato (*Republic* 606E) tells us that there were Greeks who firmly believed that Homer 'educated Hellas and that he deserves to be taken up as an instructor in the management and culture of human affairs, and that a man ought to regulate the whole of his life by following this poet'. Faced with such a judgement, on first looking into the *Iliad* or *Odyssey* one anticipates a Bible or some great treatise in philosophy, only to find two long narrative poems, one devoted to a few days in the ten-year war between Greeks and Trojans, the other to the homecoming troubles of Odysseus (whom the Romans knew as Ulysses).

Homer was a man's name, not the Greek equivalent of 'Anonymous', and that is the one certain fact about him. Who he was, where he lived, when he composed, these are questions we cannot answer with assurance, any more than could the Greeks themselves. In truth, it is probable that the *Iliad* and the *Odyssey* which we read were the works of two men, not of one. They stand at the beginning of extant Greek literature—

and hence of European letters—along with the writings of Hesiod, who lived in central Greece in the district called Boeotia. Modern students think that the *Iliad* surely and the *Odyssey* probably were not composed on the Greek mainland but on one of the islands in the Aegean Sea or still farther east on the peninsula of Asia Minor (now Turkey). And they think that the years between 750 and 700 B.C., or a bit later, were the years of this earliest literature.

For the long history of the Greeks before the time of Homer and Hesiod, the fragmentary contemporary evidence is restricted to a few thousand clay tablets in Linear B, of the fourteenth and thirteenth centuries B.C., and the mute testimony of the stones, the pottery and the metal objects unearthed by archaeologists. Intricate analysis of the remains and of place-names has demonstrated that people speaking Greek (or proto-Greek), but ignorant of the art of writing, first appeared on the scene before 2000 B.C.* Where they came from originally is not certain. In Plato's day, more than fifteen hundred years later, they were to be found scattered over a tremendous territory from Trebizond near the eastern end of the Black Sea to the Mediterranean shores of France and Libya—perhaps five or six million souls all told. These migrants were not the first inhabitants of Greece by any means, nor did they come as highly civilized conquerors overwhelming savage tribes. Archaeologists have discovered ample evidence of relatively advanced pre-Greek civilizations, some traced back well into the Stone Age, before 6000 B.C. By and large, the level of social and material development in the area was much superior to that of the newcomers. When the people whose language was Greek arrived, they came not in one mass migration, not as a single destructive horde, not in one great trek across the difficult mountain terrain of northern Greece, not as an organized colonizing expedition, but rather in a process of infiltration, perhaps punctuated by one or two more massive movements.†

* A few experts argue for a date several centuries later.
† It is significant that the bulk of the towns and districts in Greece in historical times retained their pre-Greek names.

The human mind plays strange tricks with time perspectives when the distant past is under consideration: centuries become as years and millennia as decades. It requires conscious effort to make the necessary correction, to appreciate that an infiltration would not appear to the participants as a single connected movement at all; that, in other words, neither the Greeks nor the people into whose land they came were likely to have any idea that something big and historic was taking place. Instead they saw individual occurrences, sometimes peaceable and in no way noteworthy, sometimes troublesome and even violently destructive of lives and ways of life. Biologically and culturally these were centuries of thorough intermixture. There is a clear reminiscence of the situation in the *Odyssey* (19.172-7), when Odysseus says, jumbling Greek and aboriginal names together: 'There is a land called Crete in the midst of the wine-dark sea . . . and in it are many men beyond number and ninetý cities. And there is a mixture of tongues; there are Achaeans there, and great-hearted Eteo-Cretans, and Cydonians and Dorians of the waving hair and illustrious Pelasgians.' Skeletal remains show the biological fusion; language and religion provide the chief evidence with respect to culture. The end-product, after a thousand years or so, was the historical people we call the Greeks. In a significant sense, the original migrants were not Greeks but people who spoke proto-Greek and who were to become one element in a later composite which could lay proper claim to the name. The Angles and Saxons in Britain offer a convenient analogy: they were not Englishmen, but they were to become Englishmen one day.

It was to take the Greeks more than a thousand years to acquire an agreed name of their own — and today they have two. In their own language they are Hellenes, and their country is Hellas. *Graeci* is the name given to them by the Romans and later adopted generally in Europe. In antiquity, furthermore, their eastern neighbours used still a third name for them — Ionians, the men of Yavan of the Old Testament. And all three are late, for we find none of them applied generically in

Homer. He called his people Argives, Danaans, and, most frequently, Achaeans.

The history of this nomenclature is very obscure. In Homer, Hellas is merely a district in southern Thessaly, Graia a place in Boeotia on the Athenian border. After Homer, Achaea and Argos survived but were 'downgraded' to local place-names in southern Greece. Why Hellas and Graia should have been 'upgraded' is anyone's guess, as is the reason for the Roman adoption of the latter as the generic label (also known, though not very common, in Greek writings from the late fourth century B.C. on).* It is also idle to speculate when a single name came into common use. Since nothing in the Linear B tablets provides a clue, the beginning for us is in the *Iliad*, and the presence of a common name (or names) there is a symbol that Greek history proper had been launched. But there was more that one name, and that serves as a symbol, too, of the social and cultural diversity which characterized Hellas both in its infancy and throughout its history, little though it is to be seen in the two Homeric poems.

One element, however, was remarkably stable all the time. The language with which the migrants entered Greece is classified as a member of the numerous Indo-European family, which includes the ancient languages of India (Sanskrit) and Persia, Armenian, the Slavic tongues, several Baltic languages (Lithuanian, for instance), Albanian, the Italic languages, among which are Latin and its modern descendants, the Celtic group, of which Gaelic and Welsh have retained some vitality to our own day, the Germanic languages, and various dead languages once spoken in the Mediterranean region, like Hittite (now recovered), Phrygian, and Illyrian.

For a considerable time, until about 300 B.C., Greek was a language of many dialects. But the differences among them were

* A further complication is created by the appearance of the place-name Achchiyava in several Hittite texts, of the period 1400-1200, and of a people called Ekwesh in two Egyptian documents around the year 1200. The temptation to identify both names with Homer's Achaeans has been strong (I was myself tempted in earlier editions of this book), but recent study has effectively destroyed the identification.

chiefly in matters of pronunciation and spelling, less frequently in vocabulary and syntax. Substantial though the variations were, they were not so great as to render a speaker in one dialect unintelligible to men brought up on another, probably less so than in the extreme modern instance of a Neapolitan coming to Venice. Even the artificial poetic dialect of Homer, with its Aeolic base embedded in an Ionian frame and its many coined words and forms made necessary by the metre, was apparently understood well enough by the uneducated as well as the learned all over the Greek world.

Exactly when the Greeks began to write had been a secret locked in the tablets written in Linear B; the most recent investigations suggest that the date may go back as far as 1500 B.C. The decisive point, however, came considerably later, when the Greeks took over the so-called Phoenician alphabet. With the signs came the Phoenician names for the letters, so that perfectly good Semitic words—*aleph*, an ox, *bet*, a house—were turned into Greek nonsense syllables, *alpha*, *beta*, and so on. The actual borrowing process can be neither described nor dated very closely: the evidence favours the period 800-750 B.C. The one thing that is certain about the operation is its deliberate, rational character, for whoever was responsible did more than imitate. The Phoenician sign-system was not simply copied: it was modified radically to fit the needs of the Greek language, which is unrelated to the Semitic family.

Equipped with this remarkable new invention, the Greeks could now record everything imaginable, from the owner's name scratched on a clay jug to a book-length poem like the *Iliad*. But what they wrote down and what remains today are utterly disproportionate in their bulk. Ancient literature, broadly understood to include science, philosophy, and social analysis as well as belles-lettres, faced a severe struggle for survival. The works of Homer and Plato and Euclid were written by hand on scrolls, usually of the papyrus reed. From the originals, copies were made, always by hand on papyrus or later on parchment (vellum). None of these materials is everlasting. What has survived is, apart from some accidental exceptions, what was deemed worthy of being copied and recopied for hundreds of years of Greek history and then through more hundreds of years of Byzantine history, centuries in which values and fashions changed more than once, often radically.

How little has come through this sifting process is easily illustrated. The names of some 150 Greek authors of tragedy are known, but, apart from odd scraps quoted by later Greek or Roman authors and anthologists, the plays of only three, Athenians of the fifth century B.C., are extant. Nor is that the end of it. Aeschylus wrote 82 plays, and we have 7 in full; Sophocles is said to have written 123, of which 7 still exist; and we can read 18 or 19 of Euripides' 92.* What we read, furthermore, if we read the Greek original, is a text laboriously collated from medieval manuscripts, usually from the twelfth to the fifteenth centuries of our era, the end-product of an unknown number of recopyings, and therefore always of possibly distorted transcription.

Only in Egypt did papyrus texts last indefinitely, thanks to the natural dehydration provided by the peculiar climatic conditions. Egypt came under Greek control in the empire of Alexander the Great, after which there was extensive migration of Greeks to the Nile. From the third century B.C. to the Arab conquest nearly a thousand years later, Greek was the language of letters in Egypt, and many of the papyrus finds contain literary fragments that are much older than the medieval manuscripts. In a few cases—the works of the lyric poets Alcaeus and Bacchylides, some comedies of Menander, the mimes of Herondas, Aristotle's little book on the Athenian constitution—the papyri have even brought back to light notable works that had been altogether lost. Their number is so small, however, as to underscore the fact that the process of elimination had been under way long before the monkish copyists of medieval Christendom. In the library established at Alexandria by the Greek rulers of Egypt in the third century

* The total for Euripides depends on whether or not one accepts the authenticity of the *Rhesos*.

before Christ, the greatest library of the ancient world, only 74 or 78 of Euripides's plays were available, revealing a considerable loss in the relatively short span of two centuries. At Alexandria and elsewhere scholars and librarians then resisted the process of desuetude, preserving many works in which general interest had declined or died out altogether. But after the early centuries of the Christian era there was an end even to such efforts, and the disappearance of ancient books proceeded rapidly.

The papyri of Egypt also make it abundantly clear that, in the struggle for literary survival, Homer was without a rival. Of all the scraps and fragments of literary works found in Egypt that had been published by 1963, there is a total of 1,596 books by or about authors whose names are identifiable. This figure represents individual copies, not separate titles. Of the 1,596, nearly one-half were copies of the *Iliad* or *Odyssey*, or commentaries upon them. The *Iliad* outnumbered the *Odyssey* by about three to one. The next most 'popular' author was the orator Demosthenes, with 83 papyri (again including commentaries), followed by Euripides with 77, and Hesiod with 72. Plato is represented by but 42 papyri, Aristotle by 8. These are figures of book-copying among the Greeks in Egypt after Alexander, to be sure, but all the evidence indicates that they may be taken as fairly typical of the Greek world generally. If a Greek owned any books—that is, papyrus rolls—he was almost as likely to own the *Iliad* and *Odyssey* as anything from the rest of Greek literature.*

If he were well educated, furthermore, a Greek was likely to have learned great stretches of the two poems by heart. The conservative fifth-century B.C. Athenian political leader Nicias went so far, in bringing his son up to be a proper gentleman, that he had him commit the whole to memory (Xenophon, *Symposium* 3.5). There were thinkers among the Greeks who

---

* I have compiled these figures from R. A. Pack, *The Greek and Latin Literary Texts from Greco-Roman Egypt* (2nd edn., Ann Arbor: University of Michigan Press, 1963). Not all the identifications are secure, so that some of my figures may be a little too high.

doubted that this was a good or desirable practice. To those who called Homer the teacher of Hellas, Plato replied (*Republic* 607A): Yes, he is 'first and most poetical among the tragic poets', but a proper society would bar all poetry 'with the sole exception of hymns to the gods and encomia to the good'. Two centuries earlier the philosopher Xenophanes had protested that 'Homer and Hesiod have attributed to the gods everything that is disgraceful and blameworthy among men: theft, adultery, and deceit'.* Long before Plato, he had already recognized the tremendous hold Homer had on the Greeks, and he thought that the effect was all bad.

Homer, it is essential to recall, was not just a poet; he was a teller of myths and legends. The mythmaking process had of course begun among the Greeks many centuries earlier, and it went on continuously wherever there were Greeks, always by word of mouth and often ceremonially. It was activity of the highest social (and human) importance, not just the casual daydreaming of a poet here, a more imaginative peasant there. The essential subject-matter of legend was action, not ideas, creeds or symbolic representations, but happenings, occurrences — wars, floods, adventures by land, sea and air, family quarrels, births, marriages, and deaths. As men listened to the narratives, in rituals, at festivals, or on other social occasions, they lived through a vicarious experience. They believed the narrative implicitly. 'In mythical imagination there is always implied an act of *belief*. Without the belief in the reality of its object, myth would lose its ground.'†

That may be true of savages, one may object at this point, but the Greeks were not savages. They were too civilized to believe that it was the god Poseidon who bodily prevented Odysseus from reaching his home in Ithaca, or that Zeus impregnated Leda in the guise of a swan, or that there were witches like Circe with the power to turn men into swine. These are symbolic tales, allegories, parables, perhaps dreamlike reflections of the

* Fragment 11, Diels-Kranz edition.
† Ernst Cassirer, *An Essay on Man* (Oxford University Press, 1944), p. 75.

unconscious, conveying elaborate ethical and psychological analyses and insights.

Nothing could be more wrong. Where he is able to study 'myth which is still alive' and not 'mummified', not 'enshrined in the indestructible but lifeless repository of dead religions', the anthropologist discovers that myth 'is not of the nature of fiction ... but it is a living reality, believed to have once happened'.* The Greeks of Homer's day were not primitive men, like Malinowski's Trobrianders; they lived in what is often called, by convention, an archaic society. And the Greeks of the succeeding centuries were remarkably civilized people. Yet the bitterness of Xenophanes in the sixth century B.C. and of Plato in the fourth proves precisely that, with respect to myth, many of their fellow-citizens shared the Trobriander view, or at least were closer to it than to the symbolist view. Plato himself had no doubts about the veracity of the history in Homer; it was the philosophy and morality that he rejected, the notions of justice and the gods, of good and evil, not the tale of Troy.

We must not underestimate the intellectual feat that it was for later generations to separate out the tightly interwoven strands of the Homeric tales, to re-create the Trojan War without the arrows of Apollo or the *Odyssey* without the gale-producing breath of Poseidon. Few Greeks ever attained the outright rejection of the traditional myth found in Xenophanes. Between that extreme and the primitive acceptance in full there were many intermediate points, and Greeks could be found at each. Writing after the middle of the fifth century B.C., the historian Herodotus said (2.45), 'The Hellenes tell many things without proper examination; among them is the silly myth they tell about Heracles.' That myth describes how Heracles (now better known in the Latin form, Hercules) went to Egypt, was about to be sacrificed to Zeus, and at the last moment slew all his captors. How silly, says Herodotus, when a study of Egyptian customs reveals that human sacrifice was unthinkable among them. But

* B. Malinowski, 'Myth in Primitive Psychology', reprinted in his *Magic, Science and Religion and other Essays* (New York: Anchor Books, 1954), pp. 100-1.

Herodotus had no difficulty in believing that Heracles actually existed once upon a time. In fact, he thought there had been two. Herodotus was a widely travelled man; he found what he identified as Heracles myths and Heracles cults, or parallels, everywhere, in Phoenician Tyre and in Egypt as well as among Hellenes. He tried to sift out truth from fable and to reconcile contradictions and discrepancies. Among the conclusions to which he came were that the name Heracles was originally Egyptian — for which Plutarch later accused him of being a 'barbarian-lover' — and that there were actually two figures of that name, one a god, the other a hero.

What more could Herodotus have done? The accumulated tradition of centuries of myths and legends, sacred and profane, was all that there was in the way of early Greek history. Some of it was obviously self-contradictory from the beginning. In one respect the ancient Greeks were always a divided people in their political organization. By Herodotus's time, and for many years before, Greek settlements were to be found not only all over the area of modern Hellas but also along the Black Sea, on the shores of what is now Turkey, in southern Italy and Sicily, on the North African coast, and on the littoral of southern France. Within this ellipse of some fifteen hundred miles at the poles, there were hundreds and hundreds of communities, often differing in their political structures and always insisting on their separate sovereignties. Neither then nor at any time in the ancient world was there a nation, a single national territory under one sovereign rule, called Greece (or any synonym for Greece).

Such a world could not possibly have produced a unified, consistent national mythology. In the early centuries, when myth-creation was an active process in its most vital and living stage, the myths necessarily underwent constant alteration. Each new tribe, each new community, each shift in power relations within the aristocratic élite, meant some change in the genealogies of heroes, in the outcome of past family feuds, in the delicate balances among men and gods. Obviously a new version which developed in one area did not coincide with the old, or new, version known in dozens of other areas. Nor was agreement

sought. Neither the myth-tellers nor their audiences were scholars; they were participants in their own social activities and
they were not in the least concerned with the myths of others.
It was altogether another world when a historian like Herodotus
engaged in the study of comparative mythology. Then it became
necessary to manipulate the traditional accounts—manipulate,
but not discard. They were checked for inner consistency, corrected and amplified with the knowledge acquired from the very
much older records and traditions of other peoples—Egyptians
and Babylonians, in particular—and rationalized wherever possible. Thus purified, they could be retained, as 'history' if not as
anything more.

A human society without myth has never been known, and
indeed it is doubtful whether such a society is at all possible. One
measure of man's advance from his most primitive beginnings to
something we call civilization is the way in which he controls his
myths, his ability to distinguish between the areas of behaviour,
the extent to which he can bring more and more of his activity
under the rule of reason. In that advance the Greeks have been
pre-eminent. Perhaps their greatest achievement lay in their discovery—more precisely, in Socrates's discovery—that man is
'that being who, when asked a rational question, can give a
rational answer'.* Homer was so far from Socrates that he could
not even conceptualize man as an integrated psychic whole.
Nevertheless, Homer occupies the first stage in the history of
Greek control over its myths; his poems are often pre-Greek, as
it were, in their treatment of myth, but they also have flashes of
something else, of a genius for ordering the world, for bringing
man and nature, men and the gods, into harmony in a way that
succeeding centuries were to expand and elevate to the glory of
Hellenism.

If it is true that European history began with the Greeks, it is
equally true that Greek history began with the world of Odysseus.
And, like all human beginnings, it had a long history behind it.
For history, as Jacob Burckhardt remarked, is the one field of
study in which one cannot begin at the beginning.

* Cassirer, *Essay on Man*, p. 6 (the phrasing is his, not Socrates').

Chapter 2

BARDS AND HEROES

The tale of man's decline and fall has been told in many ways. One elaborately patterned version, possibly Iranian in origin, had man destined to pass through four ages, four steps taking him further and further from justice and morality, from the paradise in which the gods had originally placed him. Each age was symbolized by a metal; in descending order, gold, silver, bronze or copper, and iron.

In due course this myth travelled west to Greece, But when first we meet it there, in the *Works and Days* (lines 156-73) of Hesiod, it has acquired an altogether new element. Between the age of bronze and the iron age of the present, a fifth has intruded.*

'But when the earth had covered this (bronze) generation also, Zeus the son of Cronus made yet another, the fourth, upon the fruitful earth, which was nobler and more righteous, a god-like race of hero-men who are called demi-gods, the race before our own, throughout the boundless earth. Grim war and dread battle destroyed a part of them, some in the land of Cadmus at seven-gated Thebes when they fought for the flocks of Oedipus, and some, when it had brought them in ships over the great sea gulf to Troy for rich-haired Helen's sake: there death's end enshrouded a part of them. But to the others father Zeus the son of Cronus gave a living and an abode apart from men, and made them dwell at the ends of earth. And they lived untouched by sorrow in the islands of the blessed along the shore of deep swirling Ocean, happy. heroes for whom the grain-giving earth bears honey-sweet fruit flourishing thrice a year. . . .'†

We do not know whether it was Hesiod or some nameless predecessor who converted the eastern myth of four ages into this

---

* Hesiod wrote 'races' (*genei*), not 'ages', but the latter is the more appropriate equivalent in a modern language.

† Translated by H. G. Evelyn-White in the *Loeb Classical Library*.

Hellenic myth of five ages. Nor does it matter, for the substance is clear. A separate Greek tradition was imposed on the importation, and the fusion was loosely accomplished. By the time the eastern myth came to Greece the Hellenes had firmly fixed in their past history an age of heroes. Under no circumstances would they surrender that brief period of honour and glory. Instead, they inserted it into the sequence of metals, leaving it to modern scholars to dig out the crudities and the contradictions and to piece out explanations.

That there had once been a time of heroes few Greeks, early or late, ever doubted. They knew all about them: their names, their genealogies, and their exploits. Homer was their most authoritative source of information, but by no means the only one. Unfortunately, neither Homer nor Hesiod had the slightest interest in history as we might understand the notion. The poets' concern was with certain 'facts' of the past, not with their relationship to other facts, past or present, and, in the case of Homer, not even with the consequences of those facts. The outcome of the Trojan War, the fall and destruction of Troy and the fruits of Greek victory, would have been of prime importance to a historian of the war. Yet the poet of the *Iliad* was indifferent to all that, the poet of the *Odyssey* scarcely less so. Similarly with the ages of man. In the Zoroastrian version there is a mathematical precision: each age was of 3,000 years, and law and morality declined by one-fourth in each. In Hesiod there is not even a whisper about date or duration, just as Homer gives no indication of the date of the Trojan War other than 'once upon a time'.

Later Greeks made up the chronology in detail. Although they did not reach entire agreement, few departed very far from a date equivalent to 1200 B.C. for the war with Troy and a period of four generations as the age of the heroes. Homer, they decided, lived four hundred years later, and Hesiod was his contemporary —in one version even his cousin.

Heroes are ubiquitous, of course. There are always men called heroes; and that is misleading, for the identity of label conceals a staggering diversity of substance. In a sense, they always seek honour and glory, and that too may be misleading without further definition of the contents of honour and the road to glory. Few of the heroes of history, or of literature from the Athenian drama of the fifth century B.C. to our own time, shared the single-mindedness of their Homeric counterparts. For the latter everything pivoted on a single element of honour and virtue: strength, bravery, physical courage, prowess. Conversely, there was no weakness, no unheroic trait, but one, and that was cowardice and the consequent failure to pursue heroic goals.

'O Zeus and the other gods,' prayed Hector, 'grant that this my son shall become as I am, most distinguished among the Trojans, as strong and valiant, and that he rule by might in Ilion. And then may men say, "He is far braver than his father", as he returns from war. May he bring back spoils stained with the blood of men he has slain, and may his mother's heart rejoice.'* There is no social conscience in these words, no trace of the Decalogue, no responsibility other than familial, no obligation to anyone or anything but one's own prowess and one's own drive to victory and power.

The age of heroes, then, as Homer understood it, was a time in which men exceeded subsequent standards with respect to a specified and severely limited group of qualities. In a measure, these virtues, these values and capacities, were shared by many men of the period, for otherwise there could have been no distinct age of heroes between the bronze and the iron. Particularly in the *Odyssey* the word 'hero' is a class term for the whole aristocracy, and at times it even seems to embrace all the free men. 'Tomorrow,' Athena instructed Telemachus, 'summon the Achaean heroes to an assembly' (1.272), by which she meant 'call the regular assembly of Ithaca'.

That in fact there had never been a four-generation heroic age in Greece, in the precise, self-contained sense of Homer, scarcely

---

* *Iliad* VI 476-81. A problem of translation may be noted here. In Homeric psychology, every feeling, emotion, or idea was attributed to an organ of the body, such as the heart or the unidentifiable *thymos*. Sometimes the feeling itself was given the name of the organ. Such phrases are scarcely translatable. I have usually rendered all these words by 'heart', to fit our customary metaphorical usage, although the sense in Homer is literal.

requires demonstration. The serious problem for the historian is to determine whether, and to what extent, there is anything in the poems that relates to social and historical reality; how much, in other words, of the world of Odysseus existed only in the poet's head and how much outside, in space and time. The prior question to be considered is whence the poet took his picture of that world and his stories of its wars and its heroes' private lives.

The heroic poem, a genre of which the *Iliad* and *Odyssey* are the greatest examples, must be distinguished from the literary epic like the *Aeneid* or *Paradise Lost*. Heroic poetry is oral poetry; it is composed orally, often by bards who are illiterate, and it is recited in a chant to a listening audience. Formally, it is at once distinguishable by the constant repetition of phrases, lines, and whole groups of lines. The coming of the day is nearly always, in Homer, 'And when rosy-fingered Dawn appeared, the child of morn'. When a verbal message is sent (and Homeric messages are never in writing), the poet has the messenger hear the exact text and then repeat it to the recipient word for word. Athena is 'owl-eyed', the island of Ithaca 'sea-girt', Achilles 'city-sacking'. Yet this is no simple, monotonous repetition. There are thirty-six different epithets for Achilles, for example, and the choice is rigorously determined by the position in the line and the required syntactical form. It has been calculated that there are some twenty-five formulaic expressions, or fragments of formulas, in the first twenty-five lines of the *Iliad* alone. About one-third of the entire poem consists of lines or blocks of lines which occur more than once in the work, and the same is true of the *Odyssey*.

Sophisticated readers of printed books have often misunderstood the device of repetition as a mark of limited imagination and of the primitive state of the art of poetry. Thus French critics of the sixteenth and seventeenth centuries placed Virgil above Homer precisely because the former did not repeat himself but always found a new phrasing and new combinations. What they failed to perceive was that the repeated formula is indispensable in heroic poetry. The bard composes directly before his audience; he does not recite memorized lines. In 1934, at the request of

Milman Parry, a sixty-year-old Serbian bard who could neither read nor write recited for him a poem of the length of the *Odyssey*, making it up as he went along, yet retaining metre and form and building a complicated narrative. The performance took two weeks, with a week in between, the bard chanting for two hours each morning and two more in the afternoon.

Such a feat makes enormous demands in concentration on both the bard and his audience. That it can be done at all is attributable to the fact that the poet, a professional with long years of apprenticeship behind him, has at his disposal the necessary raw materials: masses of incidents and masses of formulas, the accumulation of generations of minstrels who came before him. The Greek stock included the many varied and hopelessly contradictory myths that had been created in connexion with their religious beliefs and practices; all kinds of tales about mortal heroes, some fanciful and some reasonably accurate; and the formulas that could fit any incident: the coming of dawn and of the night, scenes of combat and burial and feasting, the ordinary activities of men — arising and eating and drinking and dreaming — descriptions of palaces and meadows, arms and treasure, metaphors of the sea or of pasturage, and so on beyond enumeration. Out of these building-blocks the poet constructs his work, and each work — each performance, in other words — is a new one, though all the elements may be old and well known.

Repetition of the familiar is equally essential for the audience. To follow a long and many-faceted tale, perhaps told over many days and nights, chanted in language that is not the language of everyday speech, with its metrically imposed artificial word order and its strange grammatical forms and vocabulary, is also no mean achievement, made possible by precisely the same formulaic devices that are indispensable for the creator. Poet and audience alike rest frequently, so to speak, as the familiar rosy-fingered Dawns and the messages repeated word for word roll forth. While they rest, the one prepares the next line or episode, the others prepare to attend to it.

Now it is more than probable that the *Iliad* and *Odyssey* as we know them were composed in writing, and not orally. And it is indisputable that they have a quality of genius beyond all other heroic poems, even the best of them — *Beowulf*, for instance, or the *Cid* or the *Song of Roland*. Even so, both the *Iliad* and the *Odyssey* reveal in fullest measure all the essential characteristics of unwritten heroic poetry the world over. Behind them lay long practice in the art of the bard, which had evolved the remarkable but totally artificial dialect of the poems, a dialect which no Greek ever spoke but which remained permanently fixed as the language of Greek epic. Behind them, too, lay the generations that had created the formulaic elements, the building-blocks of the poems.

With the *Iliad* and the *Odyssey* Greek heroic poetry reached its glory. Soon the bard, who composed as he chanted, began to give way to the rhapsodist, who was primarily a reciter of memorized lines, and to the hack, who prepared rehashed versions with scant literary merit. New forms composed in writing, the short lyric and then the drama, replaced the oral epic as the vehicles of artistic expression. Just when the shift occurred has been disputed by the experts without end. The view that commands more and more agreement is that the *Iliad* took the form in which we now have it in the latter half of the eighth century before Christ; and that the *Odyssey* and the poems of Hesiod came a generation or two later.

Such a dating scheme, with two Homers, some years apart, seems at first thought to be impossible. For more than two thousand years men of taste, intelligence and expert knowledge accepted the tradition that one man wrote both the *Iliad* and the *Odyssey*, and their virtually unanimous judgement had the support of the style and language of the poems, which are essentially indistinguishable apart from certain interesting preferences in vocabulary. But once the technique of ancient bardic composition was rediscovered, and with it the secret of the deceptive uniformity of style, then the differences between the two poems could be seen in their full perspective. Some of these differences had already drawn comment in antiquity. The Roman Pliny noted that there is more magic in the *Odyssey*, and he was right to a degree. In the *Iliad* the interventions of the gods have the character of minor miracles, but not even Achilles possesses magical powers, though his divine mother Thetis watches over him constantly. The *Odyssey* has similar interventions, but it also has the Circe episode, which rests on a series of magical formulas in the most precise sense and form.

A more striking distinction is to be observed in the relations between the heroes and the gods. Although decisions taken on Olympus feature frequently in both tales, in the *Iliad* the gods interfere spasmodically, in the *Odyssey* Athena leads Odysseus and Telemachus step to step. The later poem opens in heaven with Athena's appeal to Zeus to bring the hero's trials to an end, and it closes when the goddess puts a stop to the blood-feud between the hero and the kinsmen of the suitors he had killed. Even the motivation of the gods differs; in the *Iliad* it is personal, the expression of the likes and dislikes of individual deities for one hero or another, whereas in the *Odyssey* the personal element has been supplemented, in part and in still rudimentary fashion, by the requirements of justice.

The *Iliad* is filled with the action of heroes. Even when it departs from its central theme, the wrath of Achilles, its attention never wavers from heroic deeds and interests. The *Odyssey*, although shorter, has three distinct and essentially unconnected themes: the fairy-tale wanderings of Odysseus, the struggle for power in Ithaca, and the homecoming of Menelaus, Agamemnon and the other heroes. Given its location in an age of heroes, the *Odyssey* has only one proper hero, Odysseus himself. His companions are faceless mediocrities. His son Telemachus is sweet and dutiful, and when he grows up he may develop into a hero, but the poet does not take him that far. The suitors for Penelope's hand are villains — an incongruity, because 'hero' and 'villain' are not yet proper antonyms; they are not even commensurable terms; hence there are no villains in the *Iliad*. Penelope herself is little more than a convenient 'mythologically available character'.[*] Penelope became a moral heroine for later generations, the embodiment of goodness and chastity, to be contrasted with

[*] Rhys Carpenter, *Folk Tale, Fiction and Saga in the Homeric Epics* (University of California Press, 1946), p. 165.

the faithless, murdering Clytaemnestra, Agamemnon's wife; but 'hero' has no feminine gender in the age of heroes.

Finally, the *Iliad* is oriented eastward, from the vantage point of Greece, the *Odyssey* to the west. Greek relations with the west began relatively late, not before the end of the ninth century B.C., in rather tentative fashion, to become, in the following century and a half, extensive penetration and migration into Sicily, southern Italy, and beyond. The presumption is, then, that the *Odyssey* reflects this new aspect of Greek history by taking traditional materials and facing them westward. This is not to say that the travels of Odysseus in Never-Never-Land can be re-traced on a map. All attempts to do just that, and they have been numerous from ancient times on, have foundered. As the great geographer Eratosthenes said late in the third century B.C., 'You will find the scene of Odysseus's wanderings when you find the cobbler who sewed up the bag of winds' (Strabo 1.2.15). Even the topographical detail of Odysseus's home island of Ithaca can be shown to be a jumble, with several essential points appropriate to the neighbouring isle of Leucas but quite impossible for Ithaca.

Despite these differences, however, the *Iliad* and *Odyssey* stand together as against the poems of Hesiod, particularly his *Works and Days*. For all his use of the language and the formulas, Hesiod does not belong with the heroic poets. Whenever he treats of matters that are not obvious myth, when he deals with human society and human behaviour, he is always personal and contemporary in his outlook. Neither heroes nor ordinary mortals of a past age are his characters, but Hesiod himself, his brother, his neighbours, his overlords. Hesiod is wholly a part of the iron age of the present, specifically of the archaic Greek world of the eighth and early seventh centuries B.C.

Not so the *Iliad* or *Odyssey*. They look to a departed era, and their substance is unmistakably old. The *Odyssey* in particular encompasses a wide field of human activities and relationships: social structure and family life, royalty, aristocrats and commoners, banqueting and ploughing and swineherding. These are things about which we know a little as regards the period in which the *Odyssey* was apparently composed, and what we know and what the *Odyssey* relates are simply not the same. It is enough to point to the *polis* (city-state) form of political organization, widespread in the Hellenic world by then, at least in recognizably embryonic form. Yet neither poem has any trace of a *polis* in its political sense. *Polis* in Homer means nothing more than a fortified site, a town. The poets of the *Iliad* and *Odyssey*, unlike Hesiod, were basically neither personal nor contemporary in their reference.

In our present texts, each poem is divided into twenty-four 'books', one for each letter of the Greek alphabet. This was presumably a late arrangement, the work of the Alexandrian scholars. The individual books vary in length and they do not always have unity of content, although many are so self-contained that one is tempted to think of them as having been planned for recitation at a single sitting. Properly to dissect the poems, one must read them without reference to the Alexandrian division. Then it becomes clear how in the *Odyssey* the story of the Trojan War, the struggle with the suitors, and a fairy-tale, the adventures of a Greek Sinbad the Sailor, were all stitched together along with many little pieces, like the myth of the adultery between Ares and Aphrodite, myths of the afterlife, or the account of the kidnapping of a young prince and his sale into slavery (the swineherd Eumaeus). The *Iliad* may not have as obviously independent large pieces, but the snippets are innumerable. Each reminiscence and genealogical tale could have circulated, and unquestionably did, as an independent short heroic poem. The account of the funeral games for Patroclus was appropriate, with no more alteration than a change in the names, wherever the narrative required the burial of a hero. The bits of Olympian mythology fit anywhere.

The genius of the *Iliad* and *Odyssey* does not lie primarily in the individual pieces, or even in the language, for that was all a common stock of materials available to any bard in quantity. The pre-eminence of a Homer lies in the scale on which he worked; in the elegance and structural coherence of his complex narrative; in the virtuosity with which he varied the repeated, typical scenes; in his feeling for tone and tempo, his interruptions and retardations, his long similes without parallel in the history of literature—in short, in the freshness with which he both invented and manipulated what he had inherited. Paradoxically, the greater the mass of accumulated materials, the greater the poet's freedom, given a desire and the ability to exercise it. Through his genius, a Homer could create a remarkably coherent world; on the one hand different in details, and even in some essentials, from what older bards had passed on to him, and on the other hand still within the fixed path of bardic tradition, retaining a large part of that traditional world.

Merely as narrative, the *Iliad* and *Odyssey* together, for all their unprecedented length, omit very much of what was in their time becoming the accepted history of the Trojan War and its aftermath. This was a matter for free decision, for the poets knew not only the main outlines of the whole history well but also many details that they did not include, as they assumed that their audiences did too. The later monopoly of the *Iliad* and *Odyssey* easily misleads: centuries of story-telling by word of mouth, by incompetent as well as competent professionals and laymen scattered throughout Hellas, inevitably produced myriads of variants.* And other, clearly inferior epics were also composed from the traditional stock, until there was a canonical cycle of seven poems, telling the story from the creation of the gods to the death of Odysseus and the marriage of Telemachus and Circe. For a time they were all attributed to Homer, so that the Homer whom Xenophanes attacked was probably a collective name for the Trojan Cycle.† Although the incomparable qualities of the *Iliad* and *Odyssey* were early apparent, not before

---

* One of the scenes on the so-called François Vase, an elaborate Athenian basin painted by Clitias about 575 B.C. (more than a century after the composition of the *Iliad*), shows the funeral games of Patroclus, but of the five charioteers named, only Diomedes coincides with the *Iliad*'s competitors in the race.

† The long-lived Xenophanes was born about 575 B.C. The sharpness of his critique testifies to the enormous popular appeal of 'Homer' by the middle of the sixth century B.C. Towards the end of that century, Theagenes of Rhegium wrote the first recorded exegesis of Homer, and perhaps initiated the allegorical method of interpretation that later became widespread.

the fourth or the third century B.C. was it concluded that Homer did not compose the rest of the cycle as well. The other poems survived for five or six hundred years thereafter, and then they disappeared except for a few verses in quotations or anthologies.

Even if the bards who composed the *Iliad* and *Odyssey* did so in writing, the diffusion of the two poems was still primarily oral. The Greek world of the eighth and seventh centuries B.C. was mostly unlettered, despite the introduction of the alphabet. In fact, Greek literature continued to be oral for a very long time. The tragedies, for example, were surely composed in writing; but they were read by men who could be counted perhaps in the hundreds, and they were heard and re-heard by many tens of thousands all over Hellas. The recitation of poetry, heroic, lyric or dramatic, was always an essential feature of the numerous religious festivals. The origins of that practice are lost in the pre-historic era, when, on one scholarly view, some myths were a kind of ritual drama, the vivid re-enactment before the assembled people of the procession of the seasons or whatever other phenomenon inspired the ceremony. Be that as it may, in historical times a pale shadow of ritual drama had a place in the Demeter cult and other rites known collectively as 'mysteries'. But these were not the great festive occasions of dramatic performance and poetic recitation. Homer's place was in the official celebrations honouring the Olympian gods, some pan-Hellenic, others pan-Ionian, like the festival of the Delian Apollo, still others largely local, like the annual Panathenaea in Athens.* There ritual drama was absent; the gods were celebrated by other means, which invoked a less direct and less 'primitive' communion between men and the immortals.

In large part the reciters and performers were professionals, and it is one of the interesting facts of social history that in many sectors of the world they were among the first to break the primeval rule that a man lives, works and dies within his tribe or

---

* The Olympic Games were the outstanding exception. Throughout their history of more than a thousand years, the Olympic Games remained a purely athletic competition, which is significant for the extraordinary place occupied by that festival in Greek life, not as a denigration of poetry.

community. There is a hint of this in the *Odyssey* when the swine-herd Eumaeus, berated for having brought a foreign beggar to the banquet in the palace, disingenuously countered the charge with a rhetorical question (17.382-5): 'For who ever summons a stranger from abroad and brings him along, unless he be one of the craftsmen (*demioergoi*), a seer or healer of ills or worker in wood, or even an inspired bard who can charm with his song?' The frame of reference here is, of course, the private, purely secular feast, not a religious festival. But the travelling ritual player — even the organized company, such as the Arioi of the Society Islands and the Hula of Hawaii — is known from more primitive societies. Travelling artists were important in Greece throughout its history. Plato's *Ion* takes its name from a rhapso-dist, Ion of Ephesus in Asia Minor. When the dialogue opens, Ion tells Socrates that he has just come from Epidaurus, where he won first prize for his Homeric recitation at the quadrennial games to Asclepius, and that he fully expects to be equally suc-cessful in the coming Panathenaic festival in Athens.

The combination of oral transmission and lack of political centralization could in time have led to variant *Iliads*, diverging further and further from the 'original'. The temptation to tamper with the text must have been great, on political grounds alone. As the recognized authority on early history, Homer was often an embarrassment — to the Athenians, for example, whose pathetic-ally small role in the great 'national' war against Troy was increasingly incommensurate with their ascending role in Greek political affairs. But in her sharp sixth-century struggle with Megara for control of the island of Salamis, which dominates the Athenian harbour, Athens was able to justify her claim on his-torical grounds. 'Ajax', says the *Iliad* (II 557-8), 'brought twelve ships from Salamis, and bringing, he stationed them alongside the hosts of the Athenians.' To this Megara had but one answer — for neither the accuracy of Homer's history nor its relevance in territorial disputes was subject to question — and that was to charge forgery. The 'and bringing' clause, said the Megarians, was a deliberate Athenian interpolation, not part of the genuine text at all.

In the Salamis case the Alexandrian scholars in later centuries tended to agree with Megara. The forger, they thought, was Pisistratus, tyrant of Athens from 545 to 527 B.C., who, together with Solon, had taken Salamis from Megara. Far more important, it was Pisistratus who was widely reputed to have settled the problem of an authentic Homeric text once and for all by having it fixed by experts and published in a formal edition, so to speak. There was a competing tradition which assigned this role to Solon, author of the great Athenian constitutional reform of 594 B.C. In the words of Diogenes Laertius, who wrote his *Lives and Opinions of Eminent Philosophers* in the third century after Christ, but who is here quoting a fourth-century B.C. author of a *Megarian History*, it was Solon who 'prescribed that the rhapsodists shall recite Homer in fixed order, so that where the first leaves off, the next shall begin from that place' (1 57).

That there was a sixth-century Athenian recension at the root of our present texts of the *Iliad* and *Odyssey* seems to have been demonstrated from a close study of the dialect of the poems. There is some reason to accept the tradition that Pisistratus was the sponsor of that 'edition'. The attribution to Solon sounds suspiciously like a late effort to transfer the credit from a tyrant to the man who had become to the Greeks the counter-symbol, the constitutional, moderate aristocrat, at once against tyranny and despotism and against 'mob rule'.

A Pisistratean Homer poses two problems. The first and simpler of the two is this: Our present texts of the poems derive from medieval manuscripts, none earlier than the tenth century, and from numerous fragments on papyrus, a few as old as the third century B.C. How much was the text changed from the time of Pisistratus, through copyists' errors, censorship or any of the other ills that plague all ancient texts in their transmission by hand? The answer, based primarily on a comparison with the extensive quotations from Homer in Plato, Aristotle and other Greek writers, is: substantially little; and remarkably little indeed, apart from verbal changes of interest only to the philologist.

But how close was the sixth-century Athenian edition to the

original? Here we have little to go on. One thing seems sure: there was no excessive tampering with substance. The Athenian editors permitted their own linguistic habits to creep in now and then. Perhaps they even added the lines about Ajax lining up his twelve ships alongside the Athenians. But they did not consciously modernize the poems, of that we can be fairly certain, and they did not tailor the political implications in any radical way to the needs of sixth-century Athenian foreign affairs. Had they attempted to do so, they could scarcely have succeeded. The poems were already too well known and too deeply enshrined in the minds of the Greeks, and, in a sense, in their religious emotions. Besides, sixth-century Athens absolutely lacked the authority, political or intellectual, to impose a corrupted and distorted Homer on the other Hellenes. None of this is decisive, to be sure, but it permits the historian to work with his *Iliad* and his *Odyssey*, cautiously and always with suspicion, yet with a reasonable assurance that basically he is working with a fair approximation of eighth- or seventh-century poems.

Throughout all this dark history of the early transmission, public performance and textual preservation of the poems, a key role may have been played by a group on the island of Chios who called themselves the Homerids, which means, literally, the descendants of Homer. They were professional rhapsodists, organized in a kind of guild and claiming direct descent from Homer. Their beginnings are lost, but they survived at least into the fourth century B.C., for Plato writes in his *Phaedrus* (252B): 'But some of the Homerids, I believe, recite two verses on Eros from the unpublished poems.' For all we know, the Homerids may in fact have been linked to 'Homer' by kinship. Among modern Slavonic bards there are outstanding instances of transmittal of the skill within a family for several generations, and family specialization in various crafts is a common enough phenomenon in primitive and archaic societies. But it really matters little. Whether kin in fact or by accepted fiction, the Homerids were the recognized authorities on Homer for two or three centuries. And we may be sure that they would have been zealous in opposition to any effort, by Pisistratus or by anyone else, to undermine their superior knowledge and weaken their special professional position by producing a thoroughly rewritten text.

In one respect the Homerids themselves were able to introduce a false note. Commonly rhapsodists prefaced their recitations by short prologues, sometimes of their own composition. To that extent they represented a transitional form between the bard and the actor. As the acknowledged possessors of Homer's 'unpublished writings', members of the Homerid guild could claim direct Homeric authorship for the prologues they wrote. The few which are still extant were collected in later antiquity and combined with five longer myth-poems under a single title, *Homeric Hymns*, misleading in both its terms. Some of these thirty-three poems very probably originated among the Homerids in the seventh and sixth centuries B.C. The most extensive of them was addressed to Apollo; its first section closes with these highly personal lines:

'Remember me in after time whenever any one of men on earth, a stranger who has seen and suffered much, comes here and asks of you: "Who think ye, girls, is the sweetest singer that comes here, and in whom do you most delight?" Then answer, each and all, with one voice: "He is a blind man, and dwells in rocky Chios: his lays are evermore supreme." As for me I will carry your renown as far as I roam over the earth to the well-placed cities of man, and they will believe also; for indeed this thing is true.'*

Even Thucydides (3.104.4), the most careful and in the best sense the most sceptical historian the ancient world ever produced, explicitly accepted Homer's authorship of this hymn, and the personal allusion of the final lines. That was a truly astonishing error in judgement. The language of the 'hymns' is Homeric, and the comparison ends right there; they are on a lower plane not only as literature but in their conceptual world, in their view of the gods.

'For indeed this thing is true.' If the Greeks were pressed to explain how their Homer, the blind minstrel, could sing truly of events four hundred years before his time, as they believed with few exceptions, they would have pointed to tradition handed

* Translated by H. G. Evelyn-White in the *Loeb Classical Library*.

down from generation to generation, and they would have pointed to the divine spark. 'An inspired bard,' said Eumaeus the swineherd. The Greek word *thespis* means literally 'produced or shown by a god', and *thespis* provides the necessary frame of reference for the opening line of the *Iliad*: 'Sing, goddess, of the wrath of Peleus's son Achilles.'

Hesiod began his *Theogony* with a longer introduction, in which the simple invocation became a full-blown vision and personal revelation:

'And one day they (the Muses) taught Hesiod glorious song while he was shepherding his lambs under holy Helicon, and this word first the goddesses said to me . . .:

'"Shepherds of the wilderness, wretched things of shame, mere bellies, we know how to speak many false things as though they were true; but we know, when we will, to utter true things."

'So said the ready-voiced daughters of great Zeus, and they plucked and gave me a rod, a shoot of sturdy olive, a marvellous thing, and breathed into me a divine voice to celebrate things that were aforetime; and they bade me sing of the race of the blessed gods that are eternally, but ever to sing of themselves both first and last.'

Hesiod's divine voice sounds like a quotation of the *Iliad*'s description of the soothsayer Calchas, 'who knew things that were and things that shall be and things that were aforetime' (1 70). This close link between poetry and divine knowledge of the past and future found its personification in Orpheus, the sweet singer of legend in whose name a mass of mystical and magical writing piled up through the centuries. As if to underscore the point, when the Greeks came to give Homer a genealogy, as inevitably they would, they traced his ancestry back ten generations, precisely to Orpheus.

It would be wrong to turn such things aside as mere poetic fancy. When the bard Phemius said in the *Odyssey* (22.347-8), 'I am self-taught; the god has implanted in my heart songs of all kinds', to the poet and his audience that meant what it said and was to be taken like everything else in the poem, like the story of Odysseus and the Cyclops, or of Odysseus identifying himself by his ability to wield the bow no one else had the strength to pull. The witness is Odysseus himself. In the palace of King Alcinous of the Phaeacians, where the hero had appeared incognito, there was a bard named Demodocus, to whom 'God had given the art of song above all others' (8.44). After he had told various tales about the Trojan War, Odysseus said to him (8.487-91): 'Demodocus, I praise you above all mortal men, whether it was the Muse, daughter of Zeus, who instructed you, or indeed Apollo. For you sing truly indeed of the fate of the Achaeans ... as if you yourself had been present or had heard it from another.'

Still another echo is available, in a man who neither knew of Homer nor shared his inherited formulas, a nineteenth-century Kara-Kirghiz bard from the region north of the Hindu Kush: 'I can sing every song; for God has planted the gift of song in my heart. He gives me the word on my tongue without my having to seek it. I have not learned any of my songs; everything springs up from my inner being, from myself.'*

The historian's verdict, obviously, can rest neither on faith in the divine origin of the poems nor on the once common notion that sufficient antiquity is a proper warrant of truth — 'we have the certainty that old and wise men held them to be true', says the preface to the *Heimskringla*, the saga of the Norse kings. The historian, having established the point that neither the *Iliad* nor the *Odyssey* was essentially contemporary in outlook, must then examine their validity as pictures of the past. Was there ever a time in Greece when men lived as the poems tell (after they are stripped of supernatural intervention and superhuman capacities)? But first, was there a Trojan War?

Everyone knows the exciting story of Heinrich Schliemann, the German merchant with a vision and a love for the language of Homer, who dug in the soil of Asia Minor and rediscovered the city of Troy.† Some three miles from the Dardanelles, at a place now called Hissarlik, there was one of the mounds that are the almost certain signs of ancient habitation. By careful analysis of

* Quoted from C. M. Bowra, *Heroic Poetry* (New York and London: Macmillan, 1952), p. 41.
† See Appendix II.

topographical detail in ancient writings, Schliemann concluded that under this mound were the remains of the city of Ilion, which later Greeks had established on what they thought was the site of Troy and which outlived the Roman Empire. When he tunnelled into the mound he found layers of ruins, the oldest of which, we now know, dates from about 3000 B.C., and two bore unmistakable signs of violent destruction. One of these layers, the seventh according to more recent excavators, was no doubt the city of Priam and Hector. The historicity of the Homeric tale had been demonstrated archaeologically.

Schliemann's achievements were epoch-making. Nevertheless, despite the claims, the unassailable fact is that nothing he or his successors have found, not a single scrap, links the destruction of Troy VIIa with Mycenaean Greece, or with an invasion from any other source. Nor does anything known from the archaeology of Greece and Asia Minor or from the Linear B tablets fit with the Homeric tale of a great coalition sailing against Troy from Greece. No appropriate motive comes to mind. Troy VIIa turns out to have been a pitiful poverty-stricken little place, with no treasure, without any large or imposing buildings, with nothing remotely resembling a palace. It is not mentioned in any contemporary document in Hittite or any other language, nor is a 'Trojan War'. And there are other archaeological difficulties with the tale, notably in the chronology.

More interesting than the disappearance of the city is the total disappearance of the Trojans themselves. To begin with, as a nationality in the *Iliad* they are without distinguishing characteristics. True, the poet denigrates them in small, but subtle, ways that easily escape the modern reader. The Trojan hosts, but never the Achaeans, are compared to a flock of sheep or a swarm of locusts. Or, in the repeated battle incidents, a Trojan sometimes strikes a Greek with his spear, fails to pierce the armour, tries to withdraw but is slain by another warrior. Greeks also miss, but not once do the two succeeding steps follow in their case. Despite these touches, however, the Trojans are as Greek and as heroic in deeds and values as their opponents in every respect. If the opening line of the *Iliad* introduces Achilles, the closing line bids farewell to Hector, the chief Trojan hero: 'Thus they performed the funeral rites for Hector, tamer of horses.'

Hector is a Greek name (found in the Linear B tablets along with Tros and other characteristically 'Trojan' names), and as late as the middle of the second century after Christ travellers who came to Thebes in Boeotia on the Greek mainland were shown his tomb, near the Fountain of Oedipus, and were told how his bones had been brought from Troy at the behest of the Delphic oracle. This typical bit of fiction must mean that there was an old Theban hero Hector, a Greek, whose myths antedated the Homeric poems. Even after Homer had located Hector in Troy for all time, the Thebans held on to their hero, and the Delphic oracle provided the necessary sanction.

Among the Trojan allies there were peoples who were certainly non-Greek. It was for one of them, the Carians, that the poet reserved the epithet *barbarophonoi* (barbarous-talking, that is, unintelligible). The Carians are well known historically; the tomb of their fourth-century king, Mausolus, gives us our word *mausoleum*. Other Trojan allies are also historically identifiable, and that serves to underscore the curious fact that the Trojans themselves, like Achilles' Myrmidons, have vanished so completely. Even if we were to accept the ancient explanation for the disappearance of the city, that it was so thoroughly demolished by the victors that 'there is no certain trace of walls' (Euripides, *Helen*, 108) — which would involve us in new difficulties with Schliemann and his successors, who found walls — it is hard to discover a parallel for the mysterious failure of the people themselves to leave any traces.

On the Greek side there is some correlation between the important place-names given in the *Iliad* and the centres of the so-called Mycenaean civilization rediscovered by modern archaeologists, although the poverty of the finds in Odysseus's Ithaca is one of the notable exceptions. This civilization flourished in Greece in the period 1400 to 1200 B.C., and here the name of Schliemann as the first discoverer must remain unchallenged. But again Homer and archaeology part company quickly. On the whole, he knew where the Mycenaean civilization flourished, and his heroes lived in great palaces unknown in Homer's own day (but unlike the Mycenaean, or any other, palaces). And that is virtually all he knew about Mycenaean times, for the catalogue of his errors is very long. His arms bear a resemblance to the armour of his time, quite unlike the Mycenaean, although he persistently casts them in antiquated bronze, not iron. His gods had temples, and the Mycenaeans built none, whereas the latter constructed great vaulted tombs in which to bury their chieftains and the poet cremates his. A neat little touch is provided by the battle chariots. Homer had heard of them, but he did not really visualize what one did with chariots in a war. So his heroes normally drove from their tents a mile or less away, carefully dismounted, and then proceeded to battle on foot.

The contrast between the world of the poems and the society revealed by the Linear B tablets is no less complete. The very existence of the tablets is decisive: not only was the Homeric world without writing or record-keeping, but it was one in which the social system was too simple and the operations too restricted, too small in scale, to require either the inventories or the controls recorded on the tablets. Something like one hundred different agricultural and industrial occupations have been identified on the tablets; Homer knew of only a dozen or so, and it was no problem for the swineherd Eumaeus to keep them all in his head, along with Odysseus's livestock inventory. Parallels for the Mycenaean bureaucracy and its management of every facet of life are to be found in the contemporary kingdoms of the Near East, not in the Greek world at any time from Homer until after the eastern conquests of Alexander the Great.

Homer, we too easily forget, had no notion of a Mycenaean Age, or of the sharp break between it and the new age that followed its destruction. The Mycenaean Age is a purely modern construct; what the poet believed he was singing about was the heroic past of his own, Greek world, a past that was known to him through oral transmission by the bards who preceded him. The raw materials of the poems were the mass of inherited formulas and episodes, and as they passed through generations of bards they underwent change after change, partly by deliberate act of the poets, whether for artistic reasons or from more prosaic political considerations, and partly by carelessness or indifference to historical accuracy, compounded by the errors that are inevitable in a world without writing. That there was a Mycenaean kernel in the *Iliad* and *Odyssey* cannot be doubted, but it was small and what little there was of it was distorted beyond sense or recognition. Often the material was self-contradictory, yet that was no bar to its use. Poetic convention demanded traditional formulas, and neither the bard nor his audience checked the details. The man who started it all by abducting Helen is named both Alexander, which is Greek, and Paris, which is not (just as his city had two names, Ilion and Troy); he is both an easygoing sensualist and a warrior. As usual, later generations began to seek explanations, but not the poet of the *Iliad*.

We may take it for granted that there was a 'Trojan War' in Mycenaean times; more correctly, that there were many 'Trojan' wars. War was normal in that world. But a ten-year war, or a war of any smaller number of years, is out of the question. 'Would that I were in the prime of youth and my might as steadfast as when a quarrel broke out between us and the Eleans over a cattle raid. ... Exceedingly abundant was then the booty we drove out of the plain together, fifty herds of cattle, as many flocks of sheep, as many droves of swine, as many herds of goats, and a hundred and fifty bays, all mares. . . . And Neleus was glad at heart that so much booty fell to me the first time I went to war' (XI 670-84).

This was a typical 'war' as narrated by Nestor, a raid for booty. Even if repeated year after year, these wars remained single raids. There is a scene in the third book of the *Iliad* in which Helen sits alongside Priam on the battlement of Troy and identifies Agamemnon, Odysseus and a few other Achaean heroes for the old king. That could make sense at the beginning of the war; it can make none in the tenth year (unless we are prepared to believe that the poet could find no better device by which to introduce some details of little importance). It could also make sense in a brief war, and perhaps this is an illustration of the way in which one traditional piece of the story was retained after the war had ballooned into ten years and the piece had become rationally incongruous.

While the war was growing, furthermore, the bards neglected to make proper arrangements for recruits to replace the fallen men, for the feeding of besiegers and besieged, or for the establishment of some sort of communication between the battlefield and the home bases of the Greeks.

The glorification of insignificant incidents is common in heroic poetry. The French *Song of Roland* tells of a great battle at Roncevaux in the year A.D. 778, between the hosts of Charlemagne and the Saracens. Like Homer, the poet of the French epic is unknown, but he certainly lived in the twelfth century, at the time of the Crusades. Unlike Homer, he could read and he had access to chronicles, which he explicitly says he used. But the facts are these: the actual battle of Roncevaux was a minor engagement in the Pyrenees between a small detachment of Charlemagne's army and some Basque raiders. It was neither important nor crusade-like. The twelve Saracen chieftains of the poem and their army of 400,000 are pure invention, with German, Byzantine or made-up names; there is even a strong case for dismissing Roland himself as an imaginary person.* The *Song of Roland* can be checked against written records. The *Iliad* and the *Odyssey* cannot, and, in so far as historical detail is concerned, there is no way of reversing the process of distortion and re-establishing the original kernel.

The *Song of Roland* shares another negative with the *Iliad* and *Odyssey*. It is not contemporary in its social conditions, its politics or its details of war and warriors. Not that it lacks realism. On the contrary, it is of the essence of heroic poetry that, 'since heroes move in what is assumed to be a real world, their background and their circumstances must be depicted' always 'with realism and objectivity'.† Specifically, the background of Roland is the France of about a century before the poet's own time. The key to this chronological 'aberration' lies in the formulas, which have the necessary flexibility for both moving the substance along with changes in the world itself and, at the same time, restraining it from excessive contemporaneity, a limit imposed by the need to

* See P. Aebischer, 'Roland. Mythe ou personage historique?' in *Revue belge de philologie* . . ., 43 (1965), pp. 849-901.
† Bowra, *Heroic Poetry*, p. 132.

retain the 'once upon a time' image. For Homer, technical linguistic analysis has now shown that formulas were continually being lost, elaborated, and replaced, always with a certain logic. Thus, the language for the sea was ancient and stable, whereas the diction for helmets or shields remained fluid.

The world of Odysseus was not the Mycenaean Age five or six or seven hundred years earlier, but neither was it the world of the eighth or seventh centuries B.C. The list of exclusions of contemporary institutions and practices is very long and very fundamental—no Ionia, no Dorians to speak of, no writing, no iron weapons, no cavalry in battle scenes, no colonization, no Greek traders, no communities without kings. If, then, the world of Odysseus is to be placed in time, as everything we know from the comparative study of heroic poetry says it must, the most likely centuries seem to be the tenth and ninth. By then the catastrophe that brought down Mycenaean civilization and made itself felt all over the eastern Mediterranean had been forgotten.* Or rather, it had been converted into a 'memory' of a no longer existent age of heroes, proper Greek heroes. The history of the Greeks as such had begun.

Essentially the picture offered by the poems of the society and its system of values is a coherent one. Anachronistic fragments cling to it in spots, some too ancient and some, particularly in the *Odyssey*, too recent, a reflection of the poet's own time. For historical study, the institutional and psychological accuracy is easily separable from the demonstrable inaccuracy of palaces and similar material elements of the culture, and of the episodes and the narrative detail, the action. 'Homer', wrote Aristotle (*Poetics* 24.13) 'is praiseworthy in many respects, and especially because he alone of poets·perceives the part he should take himself. The poet should speak as little as possible in his own person. . . .' But this technical virtue, become a vice to poets of another world, should not mislead us, as it did no less gifted a critic than Coleridge. 'There is no subjectivity whatever in the Homeric poetry',

* The Hittites, who in the same period had ruled much of Asia Minor and exercised controls over northern Syria and Cyprus, were equally forgotten. There is no trace of them in the surviving Greek traditions.

was the judgement of Coleridge the romantic, neither the 'sub-jectivity of the poet, as of Milton, who is himself before himself in everything he wrote', nor the 'subjectivity of the *persona*, or dramatic character, as in all Shakespeare's great creations'.*

This standing at a distance from his characters and their be-haviour, which is a mark of Homeric technique, had nothing to do with indifference, with disinterest, with an unwillingness to become involved. The poet transmitted his inherited background materials with a deceptively cool precision. That enables us to treat his materials as the raw materials for the study of a real world of real men, a world of history and not of fiction. But it also besets our analysis with traps, for the temptation is ever present to ignore the implications in the poet's selectivity, conscious and unconscious, and to brush aside apparent confusions and con-tradictions in social or political matters (as distinct from narrative incidents) as nothing more than the carelessness of a bard who did not care. Real societies are never tidy: Homeric confusions in this respect are a better warrant than absolute coherence and consistency of the historicity of the picture.

Of course, there must be something of a historian's licence in pinning down the world of Odysseus to the tenth and ninth centuries before Christ. And that licence must extend still further. There are sections in the poems, such as the tale of the adultery of Ares and Aphrodite or the scene in Hades in the eleventh book of the *Odyssey*, which may have a later origin in the oral tradition than other sections. By licence, we here ignore the distinction for the most part, just as we sometimes speak of one Homer, as if the *Iliad* and *Odyssey* were the products of one man's creation. Some distortion results, but the margin of error can be held to a rather acceptable minimum, because the patterns we draw rest on an overall analysis of the poems, not on any one single verse, segment or narrative incident; because all parts, early or late, were built so much from formulas; and because later Greek history and the study of other societies together offer a great measure of control. No poet (or 'poetic tradition'), for example, could have invented

* *Table Talk*, 12 May 1830.

and described with such formal precision the institution of gift-exchange which modern anthropology has been able to parallel from other regions and continents.*

It is convenience, finally, rather than licence, that suggests retention of the ten-year war, and of Achilles and Hector and Odysseus and all the other famous names, as useful labels for unknown King X and Chieftain Y.

* See Chapter 3, and, for a remarkable and certainly independent parallel in heroic poetry, K. Kailasapathy, *Tamil Heroic Poetry* (Oxford University Press, 1968), pp. 13-15.

WEALTH AND LABOUR

In the second book of the *Iliad* the poet catalogues the contending hosts, in the case of Greeks by the names of their chief leaders and the number of ships each brought with him. 'But the multitude [i.e. the commoners] I could not relate nor name, not if I had ten tongues, nor ten mouths' (II 488-9). The list totals 1,186 ships, which, at a minimum computation, means over 60,000 men, a figure as trustworthy as the 400,000 Saracens of the *Song of Roland*. The world of Odysseus was a small one in numbers of people. There are no statistics and no ways of making good guesses, but the five-acre sites of the archaeologists, together with what is known from later centuries, leave no doubt that the populations of the individual communities were to be reckoned in four figures, often even in three, and that the numbers in the poems, whether of ships or flocks or slaves or nobles, are unrealistic and invariably err on the side of exaggeration.

One of the smallest contingents in the catalogue of ships was led by Odysseus, a mere twelve (Agamemnon had one hundred and provided sixty others for the inland Arcadians). He is announced as king of the Cephallenians, who inhabit three adjacent islands in the Ionian Sea, Cephallenia, Ithaca, and Zacynthus, together with two sites apparently on the near-by mainland. But it is with Ithaca specifically that he is always directly identified. And it is on the island of Ithaca, not in the Never-Never Land through which he later wandered, that the world of Odysseus can chiefly be examined.

The island population was dominated by a group of noble families, some of whose men participated in the expedition against Troy while others remained at home. Among the latter was Mentor, to whose watchful eye Odysseus entrusted his young wife, Penelope, who came from another district, and his only child, his newborn son Telemachus, when he himself went off.

For twenty years there was a strange hiatus in the political leadership of Ithaca. Odysseus's father, Laertes, did not resume the throne, though still alive. Penelope could not rule, being a woman. Mentor was no guardian in any legal sense, merely a well-intentioned, ineffectual figure, and he did not function as a regent.

For ten years a similar situation prevailed throughout the Greek world, while the kings, with few exceptions, were at war. With the destruction of Troy, and the great homecoming of the heroes, life was resumed in its normal ways. The fallen kings were replaced; some who returned, like Agamemnon, ran into usurpers and assassins; and the others came back to the seats of power and its pursuits. But for Odysseus there was a different fate. Having offended the god Poseidon, he was tossed about for another ten years before he was rescued, largely through the intervention of Athena, and permitted to return to Ithaca. It was this second decade that perplexed the people at home. No one in all Hellas knew what had befallen Odysseus, whether he had died on the return journey from Troy or was still alive somewhere in the outer world. This uncertainty laid the basis for the second theme of the poem, the story of the suitors.

Again there is trouble with numbers. No less than 108 nobles, 56 from Ithaca and the other islands ruled by Odysseus, and 52 from a neighbouring island kingdom, says the poet, were paying court to Penelope. She was to be forced to choose Odysseus's successor from among them. This was no ordinary wooing, ancient style or modern. Except that they continued to sleep in their own homes, the suitors had literally taken over the household of the absent Odysseus and were steadily eating and drinking their way through his vast stores; 'not twenty men together have so much wealth', according to his swineherd Eumaeus (14.98-9). For three years Penelope had defended herself by delaying tactics, but her power of resistance was wearing down. The ceaseless carouse in the house, the growing feeling that Odysseus would never return, and the suitors' open threat, made publicly to Telemachus, 'to eat up your livelihood and your possessions' (2.123), were having their effect. Just in time Odysseus reappeared, disguised as a wandering beggar. By employing all his craft and prowess, and a little magic, he succeeded in slaughtering the suitors, and, with the final intervention of Athena, in re-establishing his position as head of his household and king in Ithaca.

Abroad, Odysseus's life was one long series of struggles with witches, giants, and nymphs, but there is none of that in the Ithacan story. On the island we are confronted with human society alone (including the ever-present Athena, to be sure, but in a sense the Greek gods were always a part of human society, working through dreams, prophecies, oracles, and other signs). The same is true of the *Iliad*. For the story of the few days between the insult by Agamemnon and the death of Hector at the hands of Achilles, as for the main plot of the Ithacan theme, the nobility provides all the characters. The *Odyssey* parades other people of the island, but largely as stage props or stock types: Eumaeus the swineherd, the old nurse Eurycleia, Phemius the bard, the nameless 'carvers of the meat', the sailors and housemaids and miscellaneous retainers. The poet's meaning is clear: on the field of battle, as in the power struggle which is the Ithacan theme, only the aristocrats had roles.

A deep horizontal cleavage marked the world of the Homeric poems. Above the line were the *aristoi*, literally the 'best people', the hereditary nobles who held most of the wealth and all the power, in peace as in war. Below were all the others, for whom there was no collective technical term, the multitude. The gap between the two was rarely crossed, except by the inevitable accidents of wars and raids. The economy was such that the creation of new fortunes, and thereby of new nobles, was out of the question. Marriage was strictly class-bound, so that the other door to social advancement was also securely locked.

Below the main line there were various other divisions, but, unlike the primary distinction between aristocrat and commoner, they seem blurred and they are often indefinable. There is no generic word in the poems meaning 'peasant' or 'craftsman', and that is right. This world, as we have already seen, lacked the neatly labelled hierarchical strata of the world of the Linear B tablets or of the ancient Near East. Not even the contrast between slave and free man stands out in sharp clarity. The word *drester*, for example, which means 'one who works or serves', is used in the *Odyssey* for the free and the unfree alike. The work they did and the treatment they received, at the hands of their masters as in the psychology of the poet, are often indistinguishable.

Slaves existed in number; they were property, disposable at will. Mostly, to be precise, there were slave women, for wars and raids were the main source of supply: there was little ground, economic or moral, for sparing and enslaving the defeated men. The heroes as a rule killed (or sometimes ransomed) the males and carried off the females, regardless of rank. Before offering up his prayer for his son, Hector, who knew his own doom, said to his wife: 'But I care not so much for the grief of the Trojans hereafter ... as for yours, when one of the bronze-clad Achaeans will carry you off in tears; and you will be in Argos, working the loom at another woman's bidding, and you will draw water from Messeis or Hypereia, most unwillingly, and great constraint will be laid upon you' (VI 450-8).

Hector did not need Apollo's aid in foretelling the future. Never in Greek history was it otherwise; the persons and the property of the vanquished belonged to the victor, to be disposed of as he chose. But Hector showed gentle restraint, for his prophecy was not complete. The place of slave women was in the household, washing, sewing, cleaning, grinding meal, valeting. If they were young, however, their place was also in the master's bed, Briseis in Achilles's, Chryseis in Agamemnon's. Of the old nurse Eurycleia, the poet reports that 'Laertes bought her with [some of] his possessions when she was still in the prime of youth ... but he never had intercourse with her in bed, and he avoided the anger of his wife' (1.430-3). It was the rarity of Laertes's behaviour, and the promise of his wife's wrath, that warranted the special comment. Neither custom nor morality demanded such abstinence.

It is idle to seek for numbers here. Odysseus is reported to have had fifty female slaves, but that is surely a convenient round figure, used for the household of King Alcinous of the Phaeacians

too. A few men were also in bondage, such as the swineherd
Eumaeus, an aristocrat by birth, who had been kidnapped when
a child by Phoenician traders and sold into slavery. Male slaves
worked in the home, like the women, and also in the fields and
vineyards, never abroad as servants or orderlies.

Of the Ithacans who were neither slaves nor nobles, the bulk of
the community, some were presumably 'free' herders and peasants with their own holdings (though we must not assume that
'freedom' had precisely the same connotation and attributes as
in later, classical Greece or in modern times). Others were
specialists, carpenters and metal workers, soothsayers, bards and
physicians. Because they supplied certain essential needs in a way
that neither the lords nor the non-specialists among their followers could match, these men, a handful in numbers, floated in
mid-air in the social hierarchy. Seers and physicians might even
be nobles, but the others, though they were close to the aristocratic class and even shared its life in many respects, were de-
cidedly not of the aristocracy, as the treatment and behaviour of
the bard Phemius attest.

Eumaeus, we remember, called the élite among these specialists *demioergoi*, literally 'those who work for the people' (and once
Penelope attached the same classificatory label to the heralds).
From the word, used in the Homeric poems only in these two
passages, it has been suggested that the *demioergoi* operated in a
way well known among primitive and archaic groups, the Kabyle
of Algeria, for instance: 'Another specialist is the blacksmith, who
is also an outsider. The villagers lend him a house, and each
family pays him a fixed portion of his yearly salary in grain and
other produce.'* Unfortunately the evidence for the world of
Odysseus is far from clear or decisive. Once when Nestor, at
home, wished to make sacrifice, he ordered his servants, '"Bid
the goldsmith Laerces come here, that he may gild the horns of
the cow." . . . And the smith came, with the smith's tools in his
hands, the instruments of his craft, anvil and hammer and well-
made fire-tongs, with which he worked the gold. . . . And the old

* C. S. Coon, *Caravan: The Story of the Middle East* (London: Jonathan
Cape, 1952), p. 305.

horseman Nestor gave gold, and the smith then skilfully gilded the horns' (3.425-38). Neither the status of the goldsmith nor even his domicile is indicated here, unlike the passage in the *Iliad* about the great 'unwrought mass of iron' which Achilles offered from his booty for a weight-throwing contest. The iron was to be both the test and the prize for the winner. He will have it, said Achilles, 'to use for five full years, for neither the shepherd nor the ploughman will have to go into town for lack of iron, but this will furnish it' (XXIII 833-5).

Although nothing is ever said about remuneration, it does not necessarily follow that each family in the community gave the smith, or the other *demioergoi*, a fixed annual maintenance quota. They could have been paid as they worked, provided only that they were available to the public, to the whole *demos*. That availability would explain the word well enough.

Eumaeus indicated still another special quality of the *demioergoi* when he asked 'who ever summons a stranger from abroad ... unless he be one of the *demioergoi*' (again with a parallel among the Kabyle). Were they, then, travelling tinkers and minstrels, going from community to community on a more or less fixed schedule? Actually the logic of Eumaeus's question is that all invited strangers are craftsmen, not that all craftsmen are strangers. Some were but most were probably not, and, of those who were, none need have worked on a circuit. The heralds were certainly permanent, regular, full-scale members of the community. The bards may have wandered a bit (in the poet's own day they travelled all the time). Regarding the others, we are simply not informed.

Indispensable as the *demioergoi* were, their contribution to the quantity of work performed on an estate was a small one. For the basic work of pasturage and tillage in the fields, of stewardship and service in the house, there was no need of specialists: every man in Ithaca could herd and plough, saw and carve, and those commoners who had their own holdings worked them themselves. Others made up the permanent staffs of Odysseus and the nobles, such men as the unnamed 'carvers of the meat', who were an integral part of the household. Still others, the least fortunate, were *thetes*, unattached propertyless labourers who worked for hire and begged what they could not steal.

'Stranger,' said the leading suitor Eurymachus to the beggar (Odysseus in disguise), 'would you be willing to work as a *thes*, if I should take you in my service, on a farm at the border — you can be sure of pay — laying walls and planting tall trees? There I would furnish you ample grain and put clothes on your back and give you shoes for your feet.' Ample grain and clothes and shoes make up the store of a commoner's goods. But Eurymachus was mocking, 'creating laughter among his companions', at the direct inspiration of Athena, who 'would by no means permit the arrogant suitors to refrain from heart-rending scorn, so that the pain might sink still more deeply into the heart of Odysseus son of Laertes' (18.346-61).

A little of the joke lay in the words, 'you can be sure of pay'. No *thes* could be sure. Poseidon once angrily demanded of Apollo why he of all the gods should be so completely on the side of the Trojans. Have you forgotten, Poseidon asked, how, on order from Zeus, 'we worked as *thetes* for one year, for an agreed-upon pay', for Laomedon, king of Troy, building the wall around the city and herding cattle? And how, at the end of the year, Laomedon 'deprived us of our pay and sent us off with threats?' (XXI 441-52). The real joke, however, the utter scornfulness of Eurymachus's proposal, lay in the offer itself, not in the hint that the pay would be withheld in the end. To see the whole point we turn to Achilles in Hades rather than to Poseidon on Olympus. 'Do not speak to me lightly of death, glorious Odysseus,' said the shade of Achilles. 'I would rather be bound down, working as a *thes* for another, by the side of a landless man, whose livelihood was not great, than be ruler over all the dead who have perished' (11.489-91).

A *thes*, not a slave, was the lowest creature on earth that Achilles could think of. The terrible thing about a *thes* was his lack of attachment, his not belonging. The authoritarian household, the *oikos*, was the centre around which life was organized, from which flowed not only the satisfaction of material needs, including security, but ethical norms and values, duties, obligations and responsibilities, social relationships, and relations with the gods. The *oikos* was not merely the family, it was all the people of the household together with its land and its goods; hence 'economics' (from the Latinized form, *oecus*), the art of managing an *oikos*, meant running an estate, not managing to keep peace in the family.

Just what it meant, in terms of customary or legal obligation and in a man's own familial life, to be a permanent but free member of the *oikos* of another is by no means clear. We are not helped by the poet's aristocratic vantage-point, which normally saw more social harmony than was presumably the case in reality. Negatively, membership in the *oikos* of another meant considerable loss of freedom of choice and of mobility. Yet these men were neither slaves nor serfs nor bondsmen. They were retainers (*therapontes*), exchanging their service for a proper place in the basic social unit, the household—a more tenuous membership, perhaps, but one that gave them both material security and the psychological values and satisfactions that went with belonging. Altogether the chief aristocrats managed—by a combination of slaves, chiefly female, and a whole hierarchy of retainers, supplemented by *thetes*—to build up very imposing and very useful household forces, equipped to do whatever was required of a man of status and power in their world. The hierarchy of retainers, it should be added, reached very high indeed. As a child Patroclus was forced to flee his home. Peleus received him in his palace and 'named him retainer' of young Achilles (XXIII 90). The analogy that comes to mind at once is that of the noble page in some early modern court, just as 'lord Eteoneus, the ready retainer of Menelaus' (4.22-3) who met guests at the door and poured the wine for them, might well have been the counterpart of a Lord Chamberlain.

A *thes* in Ithaca might even have been an Ithacan, not an outsider. But he was no part of an *oikos*, and in this respect even the slave was better off. The slave, human but nevertheless a part of the property element of the *oikos*, was altogether a nice symbol of the situation. Only twice does Homer use the word that later became standard in Greek for a slave, *doulos*, which seems etymologically tied to the idea of labour. Otherwise his word is *dmos*, with its obvious link with *doma* or *domos*, a house; and after Homer and Hesiod *dmos* never appears in literature apart from a few instances of deliberate archaizing, as in Sophocles and Euripides. The treatment of the slaves looks more 'patriarchal' than the pattern familiar from plantation slavery. Eumaeus, a favourite slave, had even been able to purchase a slave for himself. To be sure, a dozen of the slave girls were hanged in the midst of the carnage of Odysseus's successful return, but it was the method of their execution alone that distinguished them from the lordly suitors, who died by the bow and the spear.

There was little mating of slave with slave because there were so few males among them. Nearly all the children born to the slave women were the progeny of the master or of other free males in the household. Commonly, in many different social systems, as among the Greeks later on, such offspring were slaves like their mothers: 'the belly holds the child', say the Tuareg nomads of the Sahara in explanation. Not so in the world of Odysseus, where it was the father's status that was determinative. Thus, in the fanciful tale with which Odysseus sought to conceal his identity from Eumaeus immediately upon his return to Ithaca, his father was a wealthy Cretan, his mother a 'bought concubine'. When the father died, the legitimate sons divided the property, giving him only a dwelling and a few goods. Later, by his valour, he obtained to wife the daughter of 'a man of many estates' (14.199-212). The slave woman's son might sometimes be a second-class member of the family, but even then he was part of that narrower circle within the *oikos* as a whole, free and without even the stigma of bastardy in our sense, let alone the mark of slavery.

Fundamentally the difference between the ordinary landowner and the noble (and then among the nobles) lay in the magnitude of their respective *oikoi*, and therefore in the numbers of retainers they could support, which, translated into practical terms, meant in their power. Superficially the difference was one of birth, a blood-distinction. At some past point, remote or near in time, either conquest or wealth created the original separation. Then it froze and continued along hereditary lines; hence the endless recitation of genealogies, more often than not starting from a divine ancestor (and therefore blessed with divine sanction). In perfect contrast, of the half-dozen or so craftsmen who are dignified with a personal name in the poems, not one has a patronymic, let alone a genealogy.

The nature of the economy served to seal and preserve the class line. Wherever the wealth of the household is so decisive, unless there is mobility in wealth, unless the opportunity exists to create new fortunes, the structure becomes caste-like in its rigidity. This was the case in Ithaca. The base of the *oikos* was its land, and there was little possibility, under normal, peaceful conditions, to acquire new land in the settled regions. Hypothetically one might push beyond the frontier and take up vacant land, but few men actually did anything so absurd and foolhardy, except under the most violent compulsions. It was not out of mere sentiment for the fatherland that banishment was deemed the bitterest of fates. The exile was stripped of all ties that meant life itself; it made no difference in this regard whether one had been compelled to flee or had gone from home in the search for land by free choice.

The primary use of the land was in pasturage. To begin the story of his adventure among the Cyclopes, which he told at the court of Alcinous, Odysseus underscored the primitive savagery of the one-eyed giants. First of all, they had not learned the art of agriculture: 'they neither plant anything nor till' (9.108). Nevertheless, Odysseus's own world was more one of pasturage than of tillage (unlike the Greek world at the time of Homer himself and of Hesiod, when agriculture had moved to the fore). Greek soil is poor, rocky and waterless, so that perhaps no more than twenty per cent of the total surface of the peninsula can be cultivated. In places it once provided excellent pasturage for horses and cattle; virtually all of it is still, in our day, good for the smaller animals, sheep and pigs and goats. The households of the poems carried on a necessary minimum of ploughing and planting, especially on orchard and vine-land, but it was their animals on which they depended for clothing, draught, transport, and much of their food.

With their flocks and their labour force, with plentiful stone for building and clay for pots, the great households could almost realize their ideal of absolute self-sufficiency. The *oikos* was above all a unit of consumption. Its activities, in so far as they were concerned with the satisfaction of material wants, were guided by one principle, to meet the consuming needs of the lord and his people; if possible by the products of his estates, supplemented by booty. But there was one thing which prevented full self-sufficiency, a need which could neither be eliminated nor satisfied by substitutes, and that was the need for metal. Scattered deposits existed in Greece, but the main sources of supply were outside, in western Asia and central Europe.

Metal meant tools and weapons, but it also meant something else, perhaps as important. When Telemachus had concluded his visit at the palace of Menelaus in Sparta, in search of news about his father, his host offered him, as a parting gift, 'three horses and a chariot-board of polished metal and . . . a fine goblet'. The young man demurred. 'And whatever gift you would give me, let it be treasure. I will not take horses to Ithaca. . . . In Ithaca there are neither wide courses nor any meadowland' (4.590-605). The Greek word customarily rendered by 'treasure' is *keimelion*, literally something that can be laid away. In the poems treasure was of bronze, iron, or gold, less often of silver or fine cloth, and usually it was shaped into goblets, tripods, or cauldrons. Such objects had some direct use value and they could provide aesthetic satisfaction, too—characteristically expressed by reference to the costliness of the raw materials and to the craftsmanship applied to them—but neither function was of real moment compared to their value as symbolic wealth or prestige wealth. The twin uses of treasure were in possessing it and in giving it away, paradoxical as that may appear. Until the appropriate occasion for a gift presented itself, most treasure was kept hidden under lock and key. It was not 'used' in the narrow sense of that word.

When Agamemnon was finally persuaded that appeasement of Achilles was absolutely essential to prevent the destruction of the Achaean forces, he went about it by offering amends through gifts. His offer included some to be presented at once, others on condition of victory. And what a catalogue it was: seven cities, a daughter to wife with a great dowry 'such as no one ever yet gave with his daughter', the girl Briseis, over whom the quarrel had broken out, seven captive women from Lesbos skilled in crafts, twelve prize-winning racehorses, and his choice of twenty Trojan women when the war was won. These, apart from the horses, were the utilitarian gifts. But Agamemnon began with none of them; first came 'seven tripods that have never been on the fire and ten talents of gold and twenty glittering cauldrons', and further on, from the anticipated Trojan spoils, as much gold and bronze as his ship would hold.* That was treasure, and its high importance is marked by the care with which it is enumerated here and again later in the poem. Menelaus's gift to Telemachus, all treasure, reappears four more times in the *Odyssey*, in three different books. The poet rarely overlooked an opportunity to revel in the value of specific gift-objects.

Whatever its purpose or its source, metal created for the individual *oikos* a special problem in the distribution of goods. For the most part distribution was internal and hence no problem at all. Since there has never been a world of Robinson Crusoes, the simplest human groups perforce have a mechanism, and it is the same one that served, with some extension, even the most elaborate princely *oikos*. All the productive work, the seeding and harvesting and milling and weaving, even the hunting and raiding, though carried on by individuals, was performed on behalf of the household as a whole. The final products, ready for consumption, were gathered and stored centrally, and from the centre they were redistributed—in the authoritarian household, by its head at a time and in a measure he deemed appropriate.

It made no difference in essence whether the family members within the household were no more than a husband, wife, and child, or whether the *oikos* was that of Nestor at Pylos, with six adult sons and some sons-in-law. The sons possessed arms and

* IX 121-56. In Plato's will, preserved by Diogenes Laertius, *Lives* 3.41-3, the itemized bequest included 'three minas of silver, a silver bowl weighing, 165 drachmas, a small cup weighing 45 drachmas, a gold ring and gold earring weighing 4½ drachmas together'. This is treasure, now narrowed to gold and silver, and like Agamemnon's it was made up indifferently of metal and metal objects.

treasure of their own, from gifts and booty, as the wives and daughters had their fine garments and jewels. But unless the males left the paternal household and established their own *oikoi*, their personal property was an essentially insignificant factor. Normally, the poems seem to say, although the evidence is not altogether clear and consistent, the sons remained with their father in his lifetime.

Architecturally the heart of the system was the storeroom. Preparing for his journey to Pylos, Telemachus 'went down to his father's spacious, high-ceilinged storeroom, where gold and copper lay piled up, and clothing in chests, and fragrant oil in plenty; and there stood jars of wine, old and sweet, filled with the unmixed drink, close together in a row along the wall' (2.337-42). And of course it contained arms and grain in quantity. More than three hundred years after Homer the Athenian Xenophon, a gentleman farmer and no tribal chieftain or king, still placed proper care of the storeroom high on the list of wifely virtues.

It was when distribution had to cross *oikos* lines that the creation of new and special devices became necessary. Wars and raids for booty, indistinguishable in the eyes of Odysseus's world, were organized affairs, often involving a combination of families, occasionally even of communities. Invariably there was a captain, one of whose functions was to act as the head and distribute the booty, all of which was first brought to a central storage point. Division was by lot, much like the division of an inheritance when there were several heirs. For example, not all of Odysseus's homecoming adventures were tragic. Two or three times he and his men had the pleasant opportunity to raid. 'From Ilion,' he began the account of his wanderings, 'the wind bore me near to the Cicones, to Ismarus. There I sacked the city and killed the men; taking the women and many goods, we divided them, so that no one might go cheated of his share through me.'*

Forcible seizure followed by distribution in this fashion, was one way to acquire metal or other goods from an outside source.

---

* 9.39-42. The final line also appears in XI 705.

Some scholars, hunting for a kernel of historical truth in the tale of the Trojan War, conjecture that it was a mass raid for essential supplies. There is not a whisper in the poems to support that interpretation, and not much else to be said in its favour, but there were no doubt small-scale wars to such a purpose, against other Greeks as well as against barbarians. However, the violent solution was neither always feasible nor even always desirable; if the aggrieved party were strong enough it invited retaliation, and there were times and conditions when even the fiercest of the heroes preferred peace. An exchange mechanism was then the only alternative, and the basic one was gift-exchange. This was no Greek invention. On the contrary, it is the basic organizing mechanism among many primitive peoples, as in the Trobriand Islands, where 'most if not all economic acts are found to belong to some chain of reciprocal gifts and counter-gifts'.*

The word 'gift' is not to be misconstrued. It may be stated as a flat rule of both primitive and archaic society that no one ever gave anything, whether goods or services or honours, without proper recompense, real or wishful, immediate or years away, to himself or to his kin. The act of giving was, therefore, in an essential sense always the first half of a reciprocal action, the other half of which was a counter-gift.

Not even the parting gift was an exception, although there an element of risk intruded. The last of the recognition scenes in the *Odyssey*, between the hero and his aged father, began in the customary fashion, with Odysseus claiming to be someone else, a stranger from another land in search of information about 'Odysseus'. Your son, he said to Laertes, visited me about five years ago and received the proper gifts. 'Of well-wrought gold I gave him seven talents, and I gave him a bowl with flower designs, all of silver, and twelve single cloaks and as many carpets and as many fine mantles, and as many tunics besides, and in addition four pretty women skilled in excellent work.' Laertes wept, for he had long been satisfied that his son had perished, and he could think of no better way to reveal that fact to the stranger than by

* B. Malinowski, *Crime and Custom in Savage Society* (London: Kegan Paul, 1926), p. 40.

commenting on the gift situation. 'The countless gifts which you gave, you bestowed in vain. For if you had found that man still alive in the land of Ithaca, he would have sent you on your way well provided with gifts in return' (24.274-85).

Then there is the interesting scene in the opening book of the *Odyssey*, in which the goddess Athena appeared to Telemachus in the shape of Mentes, a Taphian chieftain. When she was ready to part, the young man followed the expected custom: 'Go to your ship happy in your heart, bearing a gift, valuable and very beautiful, which will be your treasure from me, such as dear guest-friends give to guest-friends.'* This created a very delicate situation for the goddess. One did not refuse a proffered gift, yet she could not accept it under the false pretence of her human disguise. (Gods as gods not only accepted gifts from mortals, they expected and demanded them.) Being the cleverest of the gods, Athena unhesitatingly found the perfect solution. 'Do not detain me any longer as I am eager to be on my way. The gift, which the heart of a friend prompts you to give me, give it to me on my return journey that I may carry it home; choose a very beautiful one, that will bring you a worthy one in exchange' (1.311-8).

Telemachus had said nothing about a counter-gift. Yet he and 'Mentes' understood each other perfectly: the counter-gift was as expected as the original gift at parting. That was what gift-giving was in this society. The return need not be forthcoming at once, and it might take several forms. But come it normally would. 'In a society ruled by respect for the past, a traditional gift is very near indeed to an obligation.'† No single detail in the life of the heroes receives so much attention in the *Iliad* and the *Odyssey* as gift-giving, and always there is frank reference to adequacy, appropriateness, recompense. 'But then Zeus son of Cronus took from Glaucus his wits, in that he exchanged golden armour with Diomedes son of Tydeus for one of bronze, the worth of a hundred oxen for the worth of nine oxen' (VI 234-6). The poet's

* 'Guest-friend' is explained in Chapter 4.

† Marc Bloch, in *Cambridge Economic History*, vol. I, 2nd ed. by M. M. Postan (Cambridge University Press, 1966), p. 274, writing about the early Germanic world described by Tacitus.

editorial comment, so rare for him, reflects the magnitude of Glaucus's mistake in judgement.

There was scarcely a limit to the situations in which gift-giving was operative. More precisely, the word 'gift' was a cover-all for a great variety of actions and transactions which later became differentiated and acquired their own appellations. There were payments for services rendered, desired or anticipated; what we would call fees, rewards, prizes, and sometimes bribes. The formulaic material was rich in such references, as in the lines with which Telemachus and twice Penelope responded to a stranger's favourable interpretation of a sign from the gods: 'Stranger, would that these words be fulfilled! Speedily should you become aware of friendship and many gifts from me, so that whoever met you would congratulate you.'*

Then there were taxes and other dues to lords and kings, amends with a penal overtone (Agamemnon's gift to Achilles), and even ordinary loans — and again the Homeric word is always 'gift'. Defending himself for having lent Telemachus a ship with which to sail to Pylos and Sparta seeking information about Odysseus, a young Ithacan noble made this explanation: 'What can one do when such a man, troubled in heart, begs? It would be difficult to refuse the gift' (4.649-51). In still another category, payment for service was combined with the ceremonialism necessary to an important event. There is much talk in the *Odyssey* about the 'gifts of wooing', and the successful suitor, who reminds one of nothing so much as the highest bidder at an auction, in turn received his counter-gift in the dowry, which normally accompanied the bride. The whole of what we call foreign relations and diplomacy, in their peaceful manifestations, was conducted by gift-exchange. And even in war occasions presented themselves, as between Diomedes and Glaucus, for example, or Ajax and Hector, when heroes from the two contending sides stopped, right on the field of combat, before the approving eyes of their fellow-heroes, and exchanged armour.

Odyssean trade differed from the various forms of gift-

* 15.536-8; 17.163-5; 19.309-11.

exchange in that the exchange of goods was the end itself. In trade things changed hands because each needed what the other had, and not, or only incidentally, to compensate for a service, seal an alliance, or support a friendship. A need for some specific object was the ground for the transaction; if it could be satisfied by other means, trade was altogether unnecessary. Hence, in modern parlance, imports alone motivated trade, never exports. There was never a need to export as such, only the necessity of having the proper goods for the counter-gift when an import was unavoidable.

Laertes bought Eurycleia 'with [some of] his possessions . . . and he gave the worth of twenty oxen' (1.430-1). Cattle were the measuring-stick of worth; in that respect, and only in that sense, cattle were money. Neither cattle, however, nor anything else served for the various other, later uses of money. Above all, there was no circulating medium like a coin, the sole function of which was to make purchase and sale possible by being passed from hand to hand. Almost any useful object served, and it is noteworthy that the measure of value, cattle, did not itself function as a medium of exchange. Laertes bought Eurycleia for unspecified objects worth twenty oxen; he would never have traded the oxen for a slave.

A conventional measuring-stick is no more than an artificial language, a symbol like the x, y, z of algebra. By itself it cannot decide how much iron is the equivalent of one cow, or how much wine. In Adam Smith's world that determination was made through the supply-and-demand market, a mechanism unknown in Troy or Ithaca. Behind the market lies the profit motive, and if there was one thing that was taboo in Homeric exchanges it was gain in the exchange. Whether in trade or in any other mutual relationship, the abiding principle was equality and mutual benefit. Gain at the expense of another belonged to a different realm, to warfare and raiding, where it was achieved by acts (or threats) of prowess, not by manipulation and bargaining.

The implication that exchange rates were customary and conventional seems unavoidable. That is to say, there was no constituted authority with the power to decree a set of equations—

so much of *x* for so much of *y*. Rather the actual practice of exchange over a long period of time had-fixed the ratios, and they were commonly known and respected. Even in the distribution of booty, where a central authority, the head of the *oikos* or a king or commander-in-chief, took charge, he was obviously bound by what was generally deemed to be equitable. The circumstance that no one could punish him for flouting custom, as in the conflict between Agamemnon and Achilles, is irrelevant to the issue. For the very fact that just such a situation gave the theme for the *Iliad* illustrates how dangerous the violation could be. In this world custom was as binding upon the individual as the most rigid statutory law of later days. And the participant in an exchange, it may be added, had the advantage over the passive participant in the distribution of booty. He could always refuse to go through with the transaction if the rules were manifestly being upset, or if he merely thought they were.

None of this is to say that no one ever deliberately profited from an exchange. But the exceptional instance is far less noteworthy than the essential point that, in a strict sense, the ethics of the world of *Odysseus* prohibited the practice of trade as a vocation. The test of what was and what was not acceptable did not lie in the act of trading, but in the status of the trader and in his approach to the transaction. So crucial was the need for metal that even a king could honourably voyage in its search. When Athena appeared to Telemachus as Mentes, the Taphian chieftain, her story was that she was carrying iron to Temesa in quest of copper.* That gave no difficulties, and her visit ended with the colloquy regarding costly gifts between guest-friends.

A stranger with a ship was not always so welcome or so free from suspicion. He might have been Odysseus before Ismarus, or Achilles: 'Twelve cities of men have I destroyed from shipboard and eleven on foot, I say, in the fertile region of Troy; from all these I took out much good treasure' (IX 328-31). No wonder

---

* Neither Taphos nor Temesa is otherwise known as a place-name, and the many attempts, all failures, to identify them with one or another mining region illustrate once again the futility of such 'historicizing' of the Homeric poems.

that some Greeks eventually objected to Homer as the teacher of the Hellenes. Glorification of piracy, disapproval of theft (seizure of goods by stealth) and encouragement of robbery (seizure of goods and persons by physical prowess) — truly this seemed a world of mixed-up moral standards. 'Theft of property is mean,' protested Plato (*Laws* 941 B), 'seizure by force shameless; none of the sons of Zeus delighted in fraud or violence, nor practised either. Therefore, let no one be falsely persuaded by poets or by some myth-tellers in these matters.'

Yet there was a pattern and a consistency in the moral code; and it made sense from the premises. The distinctions rested on a specific social structure, with strongly entrenched notions regarding the proper ways for a man to behave, with respect to property, towards other men. Upon his arrival among the Phaeacians, but before he had identified himself and told of his wanderings, Odysseus was entertained by King Alcinous. Following the feast, the younger nobles competed in athletics. After a time the king's son Laodamas approached Odysseus and invited him to participate.

'Come, stranger and father, you enter the games, if perchance you are skilled in any; you seem to know games. For there is no greater fame for a man, so long as he is alive, than that which is made by foot and hand.'

Odysseus asked to be excused, pleading the heavy burden of his sorrows. Another young aristocrat then interposed. 'No indeed, stranger, I do not think you are like a man of games, such as there are many among men; but like one who travels with a many-benched ship, a master of sailors who traffic, one who remembers the cargo and is in charge of merchandise and coveted gains' (8.145-64).

The insult was unbearable under all circumstances, and to Homer's audience it must have carried an added barb when directed against Odysseus. There was something equivocal about Odysseus as a hero precisely because of his most famed quality, his craftiness. There was even a soft spot in his inheritance: his maternal grandfather, the goodly Autolycus, 'surpassed all men in thievishness and the oath, for that was a gift to him from the god Hermes' (19.395-7). Later the doubts of many Greeks turned to open contempt and condemnation. 'I know full well,' said Philoctetes in the Sophoclean play of that name (lines 407-8), 'that he would attempt with his tongue every evil word and villainy.' What saved the Homeric Odysseus was the fact that his guile was employed in the pursuit of heroic goals; hence Hermes, the god of tricks and stealth, may have given him the magic with which to ward off Circe the witch, but it was Athena who was his protector and his inspiration in his heroic exploits. To the insult in Phaeacia he first replied with an indignant speech, but Odysseus, of all men, could not establish his status with words. Having finished his reply, he leaped up, seized a weight greater than any the young men had cast, and, without removing his garment, threw it far beyond their best mark.

Possibly there were men, a very few from among those who were not men of games, living in the interstices of society, who travelled in many-benched ships and trafficked. Yet there is no single word in either the *Iliad* or the *Odyssey* that is in fact a synonym for 'merchant'. By and large, the provisioning of the Greek world with whatever it obtained from the outside by peaceful means was in the hands of non-Greeks, the Phoenicians in particular. They were really a trading people, who sailed from one end of the known world to the other, carrying slaves, metal, jewellery, and fine cloth. If they were motivated by gain — 'famed for ships, greedy men' (15.415-6) — that was irrelevant to the Greeks, the passive participants in the operation.

The need for metal, or any similar need, was an *oikos* affair, not an individual matter. Its acquisition, whether by trade or by raid, was therefore a household enterprise, managed by the head. Or it could be larger in scale, involving many households acting cooperatively. Internally, the situation was altogether different. Trade within the household was impossible by definition: the *oikos* was a single, indivisible unit. Because a large sector of the population was enmeshed in the great households, they too were withdrawn from any possibility of trade, external or internal. The *thetes*, finally, were absolutely excluded; having nothing, they had nothing to exchange.

That leaves the non-aristocratic, small-scale herders and peasants. In their households shortages were chronic, if not absolute as a consequence of a crop failure or a disaster to their flocks, then partial because of an imbalance in the yield. Their troubles are not the subject of heroic poetry, and neither the *Iliad* nor the *Odyssey* is informative in this regard. The inference is permissible, however, that some of their difficulties were alleviated by barter, primarily with one another, and without the instrumentality of a formal market, absolutely unknown in this world. They exchanged necessities, staples, undoubtedly on the same principles of equivalence, ratios fixed by custom, and no gain.

Herders and peasants, including the *thetes*, always had another resource to draw upon. They could work. Unlike trade, skill with the hands, labour, was never greeted with contempt in the poems; in that area, the society's moral judgement was directed not to the act itself but to the person and the circumstance. Back in Ithaca, but still disguised as a beggar, Odysseus, in reply to Eurymachus's mocking offer of employment, challenged the suitor to a ploughing contest — just as, in his proper guise, he boasted of his superior bowmanship or his weight throwing. But Odysseus was not required to plough in order to live. In fact, it is obvious that, though he knew how to till and herd and build a raft, he rarely did any work on his estate except in sport. That was the great dividing-line between those who were compelled to labour and those who were not. Among the former, the men with the inspired skills, the bards and the metalworkers and the others, were an élite. Above all, the test was this, that 'the condition of the free man is that he does not live under the constraint of another'.* Hence there was a line between those who, though they worked, remained more or less their own masters as independent herders and peasants, and on the other side the *thetes* and the slaves who laboured for others, whose livelihood was not in their own hands. The slaves, at least, were usually the victims of chance. The *thes* was in a sense the worst of all: he voluntarily contracted away his control over his own labour, in other words, his true freedom.

* Aristotle, *Rhetoric* 1367a32, writing with specific reference to labour.

71

Much of the psychology of labour, with its ambivalence between admiration of skill and craft and its rejection of the labourer as essentially and irretrievably an inferior being, found its expression on Olympus. Having humanized the gods, the bard was consistent enough to include labour among the heavenly pursuits. But that entailed a certain difficulty. Zeus the insatiable philanderer, Apollo the archer who was also a minstrel, Ares the god of battle—these were all embodiments of noble attributes and activities, easily re-created in man's image. But how could the artisan who built their palaces and made their weapons and their plate and their ornaments be placed on equal footing with them, without casting a shadow over the hierarchy of values and status on which society rested? Only a god could make swords for gods, yet somehow he must be a being apart from the other gods.

The solution was neatly turned, very neatly indeed. The divine craftsman was Hephaestus, son of Hera. His skill was truly fabulous, and the poet never tired of it, lingering over his forge and his productions as he never sang of the smith in Ithaca. That was the positive side of the ambivalence. The other was this: of all the gods, Hephaestus alone was 'a huge limping monster' with 'a sturdy neck and hairy chest' (XVIII 410-5). Hephaestus was born lame, and he carried the mark of his shame on his whole personality. The other gods would have been less than human, in consequence, were Hephaestus not to be their perennial source of humour. Once, when Zeus and Hera were having a fearful quarrel, the limping god attempted the role of peacemaker, filling the cups with nectar for all the assemblage. 'And unquenchable laughter was stirred up among the blessed gods as they watched Hephaestus bustling about the palace' (I 599-600). And the social fabric of the world of Odysseus was saved.

In fact, the mirror-image on Olympus was still more subtle. In art and craftsmanship, Athena was frequently linked with Hephaestus, as in the simile in which a comparison is drawn with a goldsmith, 'a skilful man whom Hephaestus and Pallas Athena taught all kinds of craft (*techne*)' (6.232-4). But there was absolutely nothing deformed or the least bit comical about Athena, deservedly her father's favourite among the gods. It was unnecessary to apologize for Athena's skill with her hands, for the pattern with respect to work differed somewhat for women. Denied the right to a heroic way of life, to feats of prowess, competitive games, and leadership in organized activity of any kind, women worked, regardless of class. With her maids, Nausicaa, daughter of the Phaeacian king, did the household laundry. Queen Penelope found in her weaving the trick with which to hold off the suitors. Her stratagem, however, of undoing at night what she had woven in the day, repeated without detection for three full years until one of her maids revealed the secret, suggests that her labour was not exactly indispensable. The women of the aristocracy, like their men, possessed all the necessary work skills, and they used them more often. Nevertheless, their real role was managerial. The house was their domain, the cooking and washing, the cleaning and the clothes-making. The dividing-line for them was rather in the degree to which they performed the chores themselves—between those who supervised, working only to pass the time, and those whom circumstances compelled to cook and sew in earnest.

Chapter 4

HOUSEHOLD, KIN, AND COMMUNITY

The subject of heroic poetry is the hero, and the hero is a man who behaves in certain ways, pursuing specified goals by his personal courage and bravery. However, the hero lives in, and is moulded by, a social system and a culture, and his actions are intelligible only by reference to them. That is true even when the poet's narrative appears to ignore everything and everyone but the heroes.

No one who reads the *Iliad* can fail to be struck by the peculiar character of the fighting. There are tens of thousands of soldiers on hand, yet the poet has eyes only for Ajax or Achilles or Hector or Aeneas. In itself, such a literary device is commonplace; it is a very rare artist who has both reason and genius enough to re-create masses of men in battle. Nor is there historical objection to the individual combat between champions, as between Achilles and Hector, or, even more interesting in some ways, between Ajax and Hector, ending in a draw and an exchange of gifts. The false note comes in the full-scale fighting. There the confusion is indescribable. No one commands or gives orders. Men enter the battle and leave at their own pleasure; they select their individual opponents; they group and regroup for purely personal reasons. And the disorganization, unlike the chaotic movements in a war novel like Stephen Crane's *The Red Badge of Courage*, does not stem from the breakdown of an original plan of action but from the poet's concentration on his heroes as individuals. He must bring in the army as a whole to maintain the necessary realism of the war story, but he returns to the central figures as quickly as possible.

Off the field of battle there are hundreds of small details essentially irrelevant to either the narrative or the action of the heroes. The hanging of the twelve slave girls, Mentes's cargo of iron, the purchase of Eurycleia by Laertes, Telemachus's visit to the storeroom—these odd bits are too fragmentary to have interest as independent scenes, and in a sense they are all unnecessary for the movement of the tale. Yet the poet introduces them on every page, briefly, in a few phrases or lines, but with the greatest skill and attention. Both the artistry of the narrative and the conviction with which it was received rest in large measure on these incidentals. They underscore or elucidate behaviour, they give colour to the proceedings, they remind the audience again and again of the truthfulness of the account. And today they make accessible the complicated social system and its values.

In the action of the individual heroes, status was perhaps the main conditioning factor. A man's work and the evaluation of his skills, what he did and what he was not to do in the acquisition of goods and their disposition, within the *oikos* and without, were all status-bound. It was a world of multiple standards and values, of diversified permissions and prohibitions. With respect to work and wealth, we have seen, the determinant was always the particular social grouping to which one belonged, not the skills, desires or enterprise of an individual. The chief heroes were individuals, not robots. Nevertheless, in all their behaviour, by no means in the economic sphere alone, the implicitly indicated limits to tolerable individual initiative and deviance were extremely narrow: among the nobles, only in the degree of one's strength and prowess, the magnitude of one's ambition for glory, and the development of one's sense of what was fitting. There were variations in temperament, too, like Odysseus's outstanding craftiness or Achilles's excessively forthright responses, but they were more puzzling than not.

Agamemnon is a convenient illustration of the far-reaching effects of status. He is several times called 'most kingly' of the heroes at Troy, clearly not in sarcasm, yet he was by no means the most heroic in his personal capacities or accomplishments. His position at the head of the invading forces was not personally earned but was the consequence of the superior position in power he had inherited, as the leader who could bring the largest contingent, one hundred ships. His status gave him command, hence the right to distribute the booty and select the prize of honour. His status also prevented the aggrieved Achilles from expressing defiance other than in the passive form of a mighty sulk, though in valour Achilles was the admitted superior.

Or consider Telemachus. He was still a youngster, to be sure, yet there was unmistakable irritation in Athena's 'You ought not continue your childish ways, now that you are no longer of an age' (1.296-7). Maturity was more than chronological; a twenty-year-old of such lineage and class was expected to grow faster and further, and to respond sooner to circumstances requiring adult behaviour.

Athena was prodding Telemachus hard because of the grave situation created by the suitors. She pointed to Orestes as a model. 'Have you not heard what fame illustrious Orestes received among all men when he killed his father's murderer, wily Aegisthus?'* Penelope's suitors had committed no murder, nor were they threatening one (later they tried unsuccessfully to ambush and assassinate Telemachus). Nevertheless, Orestes was a proper model for Odysseus's son, altogether apart from the hero-theme of glory and honour. Both young men faced obligations of the same species, namely, those that stemmed from the family, the one to avenge his father's death, the other to preserve his paternal *oikos*.

Orestes and Aegisthus, Telemachus and all 108 suitors were nobles. Within that single social class, however, there was another kind of group relationship and group loyalty, the family bond. Agamemnon, it may be noted, was supported in his right to lead the Greek armies by the fact that his brother Menelaus was the aggrieved party to be avenged. When criminal acts were involved, the family, not the class (or the community as a whole), was

---

* 1.298-300. Whenever Orestes is mentioned in the *Odyssey* it is never said explicitly that he also killed his mother Clytaemnestra. Yet that is the central theme of the Orestes tragedy in Greek drama. However one explains Homer's silence, the contrast, and the obviously contemporary matter in the plays, notably the court scenes, indicate once again that information taken from post-Homeric treatment of the old myths is worse than useless in a study of the world of Odysseus. Later poets and playwrights reworked the materials freely, and with total unconcern for history.

charged with preserving the standards of conduct and with punishing any breach.

Historically there is an inverse relationship between the extension of the notion of crime as an act of public malfeasance and the authority of the kinship group. Primitive societies are known in which it is not possible to find any 'public' responsibility to punish an offender. Either the victim and his relations take vengeance or there is none whatsoever. The growth of the idea of crime, and of criminal law, could almost be written as the history of the chipping away of that early state of family omnipotence. The crumbling process had not advanced very far by the time of Orestes and Telemachus, nor did it begin in the places modern Western man, with his own peculiar ethical traditions, would surely have selected. Homicide, as the most obvious example, remained largely a private affair. Much as the collective conscience may have thought punishment desirable, it failed to provide any instrumentality outside of the kinsmen. They in turn refused to distinguish among homicides as between a justified one and a malicious one. Odysseus's slaughter of the suitors brought their fathers and relations to arms. 'For this is dishonour,' said Antinous's father (24.433-5), 'even for those who come after to hear, if we do not avenge the murder of our sons and brothers.' Had Athena not intervened to close the poem, as she opened it, no human force in Ithaca could have prevented still more bloodshed.

The profundity of the Greeks' kinship attachment, throughout their history, is immediately apparent from their passion for genealogies. That never changed radically at any time. The language of family was altered, however, and the tendency was towards narrowing the circle. Homer has a special word, *einater*, for a husband's brother's wife, to cite a clear-cut example, and that word soon disappeared from the ordinary vocabulary. The reason for the change is not hard to find. In a household like Nestor's there were half a dozen women whose relationship to one another was that of husband's brother's wife. When that kind of extended family unit disappeared, when daughters went off to their husband's homes and sons set up their own establishments while the father still lived, the fine distinction of *einater* became super-fine. The more general word *kedestes* for every in-law was then good enough.

The coexistence of three distinct but overlapping groups, class, kin and *oikos*, was what defined a man's life, materially and psychologically. The demands of each of the three did not always coincide; when they conflicted openly there were inevitable tensions and disequilibriums, And then there was still a fourth group in the picture. Once Athena had put a little backbone into Telemachus he, still at her suggestion, summoned the Ithacans to an assembly. The first speaker, an old noble Aegyptius, asked who had called the meeting and on what business. In reply Telemachus repeated the phrasing of the question in part when he said, 'Neither have I heard any news that the army [i.e. Odysseus and his men] is returning . . . nor do I disclose or speak of any other public matter.' Then he added, 'But of my own matter, for an evil has fallen on my household, a double one' (2.42-6).

The twin evils were Odysseus's failure to return and the suitors' refusal to clear out. The suitors were altogether Telemachus's private business. But old Aegyptius thought that the meeting had been called on a public matter, and the very existence of such a notion is significant. The assembly (*agora*)* was unknown among the Cyclopes; that was the second item listed by Odysseus as a sign of their wholly uncivilized state (the absence of *themis* was the third).† An assembly is no simple institution. As a precondition it requires a relatively settled, stable community made up of many households and kinship groups; in other words, the imposition upon kinship of some territorial superstructure. That means that the several households and larger family groups had

---

* 'Assembly' is the original sense of *agora*, both the place of meeting and the meeting itself. The market-place connotation, with which it is most commonly associated in the modern mind, is very much later. There is not a trace of it in Homer.

† *Themis* is untranslatable. A gift of the gods and a mark of civilized existence, sometimes it means right custom, proper procedure, social order, and sometimes merely the will of the gods (as revealed by an omen, for example) with little of the idea of right.

substituted for physical coexistence at arm's length a measure of common existence, a community, and hence a partial surrender of their own autonomy. In this new and more complex structure of society a private affair was one that remained within the sole authority of the *oikos* or kinship group, a public matter one in which the decision was for the heads of all the separate groups to make, consulting together.

Neither the beginnings nor the early history of the Greek community can be described. The original Greek migrants into the eastern Mediterranean region were not primitive hunters. They were a pastoral people who, so the signs seem to say, had learned the art of agriculture as well. Apparently their organization was tribal, modified by temporary expedients while they were on the move. But the world they entered was far more complex, especially so on its perimeter, where, in Egypt and the Near East, there had already been a long experience in large-scale territorial organization. In the thousand years, roughly, that ensued until the age of Odysseus, social and political organization had a relatively complicated history. There was no standing still for a thousand years; nor was the movement all in a straight line or all in one direction, up or down. These were centuries filled with violent upheavals and catastrophes, leaving clear if not very legible imprints on the archaeological record. When they occurred with sufficient force they brought down institutions along with the stone walls and the lives of men.

Odysseus's Ithaca was more household- and kinship-bound, less integrally a civic community, than many a civilized centre of earlier centuries. We are led to the conclusion that the widespread physical destruction in Greece in the period about 1200 B.C. (which extended to other areas of the eastern Mediterranean) also carried away much of the existing political structure and replaced it by the unbounded kinship principle. There is the further implication, however, that the slow return of the community was no longer a new thing among the heroes of the poems, that *agora* and *themis*, and the idea that there were both public and private matters, were well established in their thinking. The assembled Ithacans were puzzled by several aspects of Telemachus's summons; there is no sign of discomfort or uncertainty in how to go about the business of an assembly.

The rules were rather simple. The assembly was normally summoned by the king at his pleasure, without advance notice. When the men were abroad on a campaign, an assembly could be called in the camp to consider matters pertaining to the war.* At home or in the field there were no stated meeting dates, no fixed number of sessions. In Odysseus's absence, Ithaca had gone more than twenty years without a meeting, yet others were seemingly empowered to call one had they so wished, just as Achilles once assembled the Achaeans in the field although Agamemnon, not he, was commander-in-chief. Aegyptius's query in Ithaca implied no doubt about the validity of the assembly summoned by Telemachus; the old man was merely curious to know who had broken the twenty-year silence.

The usual time of meeting was dawn. 'And when rosy-fingered Dawn appeared, the child of morn, the dear son of Odysseus rose from his bed and put on his garments. . . . Straightway he bade the clear-voiced heralds summon the long-haired Achaeans to an assembly. They made the call, and the latter gathered swiftly indeed' (2.1-8). The one item on the agenda was the issue the summoner wanted discussed. Whoever felt moved to speak rose to do so, and while he talked he held the sceptre placed in his hand by the herald — in a quite literal sense a magic wand that rendered the speaker physically inviolate. Custom gave the eldest the first opportunity to take the floor. Thereafter the sequence was determined by the course of the debate rather than by a fixed seniority system. And when there were no more speakers the meeting dissolved.

The assembly neither voted nor decided. Its function was twofold: to mobilize the arguments pro and con, and to show the king or field commander how sentiment lay. The sole measure of opinion was by acclamation, not infrequently in less orderly forms, like the shouting down of an unpopular presentation. The king was free to ignore the expression of sentiment and go

* At the end of the third century B.C. a meeting of the armed levy of the Aetolian League sometimes functioned as a regular assembly of the League.

his way. That, in fact, was what introduced the theme for the
Iliad. A priest had come to the Achaean camp to ransom his
captive daughter Chryseis. He made a brief plea and 'all the
other Achaeans assented by acclamation to reverence the priest
and to accept the splendid ransom; but it did not please the
heart of Atreus's son Agamemnon and roughly he sent him
away'.* In great anger the god Apollo came down from Olympus
and for nine days poured arrows into the Achaean host, 'and the
close-set pyres of the dead burned continuously', until Hera took
pity and bade Achilles summon an assembly. There Agamemnon,
in a violent quarrel with Achilles, bowed to Apollo, agreed to
release the priest's daughter, and then made the personal, uni-
lateral decision to replace her in his hut with Briseis, the prize
among Achilles's captives.

Achilles spoke six times at the meeting, Agamemnon four, but
throughout they addressed each other directly, like two men
wrangling in the privacy of their homes. Once Agamemnon in-
terrupted what he was saying to Achilles, turned to the assemblage, and announced his decision to surrender Chryseis and the
procedure to be followed to appease the god. Apart from this
one moment, the disputants talked only to each other. When
Nestor intervened near the end to urge peace between them, he
too spoke only to the two heroes. Finally, 'when the two had
finished fighting with quarrelsome words, they dissolved the
assembly beside the ships of the Achaeans' (i 304-5). In this
instance, unlike others in the *Iliad*, the army indicated no preference or sentiment of any kind.

Such a performance and so informal an institution as this sort
of assembly are not easily evaluated in parliamentary terms. A
king or commander-in-chief was under no compulsion to call a
meeting, and yet the aristocracy, and in a certain sense even the
people, had a right to be heard, for otherwise no one other than
the king could have issued a summons. The chief nobles serve
the king as a council of elders, and again there was nothing binding about their recommendations. On one occasion, for example,
King Alcinous assembled the Phaeacian 'chieftains and leaders',

* i 22-5, repeated i 376-9.

informed them of his decision to have Odysseus convoyed to Ithaca, and then led him to the feast, without even a pause for their comment or reaction.

Nevertheless, the *Iliad* and *Odyssey* are filled with assemblies and discussions, and they were not mere play-acting. Viewed from a narrow conception of formal rights, the king had the power to decide, alone and without consulting anyone. Often he did. But there was *themis* — custom, tradition, folk-ways, *mores*, whatever we may call it, the enormous power of 'it is (or is not) done'. The world of Odysseus had a highly developed sense of what was fitting and proper. Only once in either poem did a commoner, Thersites, a man without a claim to a patronymic, presume to take the floor at an assembly, and he was promptly beaten down by Odysseus. Thersites behaved improperly: the people acclaimed or dissented as they listened, they did not themselves make proposals. That was a prerogative of the aristocrats; it was their role to advise, the king's to take heed if he would. 'It behoves you,' Nestor told Agamemnon at a meeting of the elders, 'more than anyone both to speak words and to listen' (IX 100). The king who ignored the prevailing sentiment was within his right, but he ran a risk. Any ruler must calculate on the possibility that those bound by law or custom to obey him may one day refuse, by passive resistance or outright revolt. The Homeric assembly thus provided the kings with a test of public opinion, as the council of elders revealed the sentiment among the nobles.

A large measure of informality, of fluidity and flexibility, marked all the political institutions of the age. There were lines of responsibility and power, and they were generally understood, but they often crossed and then there was trouble. If the king in assembly could ignore its opinion, no matter how clear and unanimous, it was equally true that the Greek world got along as well as ever without kings for ten years — and Ithaca for twenty. This was possible because the superimposition of a community, the territorial unit under a king, upon the household-kinship system merely weakened the dominant position of the latter, but only in part and only in certain respects. Primarily it was war, defensive in particular, which was an activity of the community, while the usual pursuits of peace, the procurement of sustenance, social intercourse, the administration of justice, relations with the gods, and even non-bellicose relations with the outside world, were largely conducted, as before, through the interlocking channels of *oikos*, kin and class.

And kinship thinking permeated everything. Even the relatively new, non-kinship institutions of the community were shaped as much as possible in the image of the household and the family. The perfect symbol, of course, was the metaphor of the king as father (on Olympus, Zeus was called 'father of the gods', which, taken literally, he was of some but not of others). In certain of his functions — in the assembly, for example, or in offering sacrifices to the gods — the king in fact acted the patriarch. The Greek verb *anassein*, which means 'to be a lord', 'to rule', is used in the poems for both the king (*basileus*) and the head of an *oikos* with almost complete indifference. It is equally applicable to the gods; Zeus, for instance, 'rules (*anassein*) over gods and men' (e.g. ii 669).

To rule, after all, is to have power, whether over things, over men (by other men or some god), or over men and gods together (by Zeus). But the bardic formulas sometimes add a little touch that is extremely revealing. In five instances *anassein* is qualified with the adverb *iphi*, 'by might', so that king's rule (but never the householder's) becomes rule by might. This must under no circumstances be taken to imply tyranny, forcible rule in the invidious sense. When Hector prayed for his son to 'rule by might in Ilion' (vi 478), he was asking the gods that the boy succeed to the throne, not that he be endowed with the qualities of a despot. And when Agamemnon named one daughter Iphianassa, he was calling her 'princess', just as Iphigenia, 'mightily born', indicates royal birth.

Iphi quietly directs attention to the limits upon the parallel between head of a household and king. One critical test lay in the succession. The kings, like Hector, were personally interested in pushing the family parallel to the point at which their sons could automatically follow them on the throne as they succeeded them in the *oikos*. 'The king is dead! Long live the king!' That proclamation is the final triumph of the dynastic principle in monarchy. But never in the world of Odysseus was it pronounced by the herald. Kingship had not come that far, and the other aristocrats often succeeded in forcing a substitute announcement: 'The king is dead! The struggle for the throne is open!' That is how the entire Ithacan theme of the *Odyssey* can be summed up. 'Rule by might', in other words, meant that a weak king was not a king, that a king either had the might to rule or he did not rule at all.

In one of his frequent taunting interchanges with the suitors, Telemachus spoke rather curiously: 'After all, here in sea-girt Ithaca there are many other kings (*basileis*) among the Achaeans, young and old, one of whom may take the place, since illustrious Odysseus is dead' (1.394-6). This remark is different from Nestor's calling Agamemnon 'most kingly', for there the comparison was with the assembled heroes at Troy, many of whom were in fact kings, whereas here Telemachus meant the nobles of Ithaca, not one of whom was a king. Were this a unique passage, it could be ignored as a first crude effort on the part of Telemachus, whose growing-up process had begun on the same day, to imitate the guile of his father. But the oscillation between *basileus* as king and *basileus* as chief—that is, as head of an aristocratic household with its servants and retainers—is duplicated elsewhere in the Homeric poems and by other early writers. Nor is this an instance of poverty of language. Behind the terminology can be felt all the pressure of the aristocracy to reduce kingship to a minimum. Aristocracy was prior to kingship logically, historically, and socially. While recognizing monarchy, the nobles proposed to maintain the fundamental priority of their status, to keep the king on the level of a first among equals.

The fundamental conflict is laid bare in all its complexity in the opening book of the *Odyssey*. Telemachus's reference to the many kings in Ithaca was said in his reply to a challenge by the suitor Antinous: 'Never may Cronion [i.e. Zeus] make you king in sea-girt Ithaca, which is your partimony by birth.' Telemachus sadly conceded the probable truth of that hope and prophecy, and went on to demand that his household, as distinct from the kingship, be returned to him. 'Telemachus,' was the answer of another suitor, the more guileful Eurymachus, 'it really lies in the lap of the gods, who shall be king of the Achaeans in sea-girt Ithaca. But you may keep your own property and be lord (*anassein*) in your house' (1.386-402). Let Penelope choose Odysseus's successor as spouse, and peace would be restored in Ithaca. The successful suitor would take the throne and Telemachus could 'with pleasure enjoy all [his] patrimony, eating and drinking, while she attends to the house of another' (20.336-7). Otherwise the daily feasting would continue in this curious war of attrition, until one day Telemachus would find himself with no household worth inheriting.

The element of naked force was not at all disguised. The decision might ultimately lie with the gods, but heroes were obligated to try to direct it by the power of their arms. In the futile assembly that Telemachus summoned on the following day, Leocritus openly and bluntly warned that 'if Odysseus of Ithaca himself were to come and were eager in his heart to drive from the palace the noble suitors who feast in his house, yet his wife would find no pleasure in his coming, though she yearns for him. On the contrary, just there would he meet with evil destiny, were he to fight against greater numbers' (2.246-51).

Leocritus was a poor prophet. But the fact is that when Odysseus returned there was no automatic resumption of his royal position. He had to fight against heavy odds and with all his powers of strength and guile to regain his throne. Leocritus had overlooked one matter, the interest of Athena in Odysseus. 'I should surely have perished in my palace of the evil fate of Agamemnon son of Atreus, had not you, goddess, told me each thing rightly' (13.383-5).

It may be protested that all this is to read historical significance into what is no more than the story line of the poem. Had Odysseus not returned, we should have had no *Odyssey*; had he met the fate from which the goddess rescued him, we should have had an altogether different tale. True; but we must remember that Odysseus is our conventional name for King X. Stripped of the details of myth and narrative, the diversified homecomings are precisely what would have occurred in this world, with its delicate, easily upset balance of powers. Nestor and Menelaus smoothly picked up the threads as they had been before the expedition, although each in different personal circumstances; Agamemnon was murdered by Aegisthus, his successor as spouse, master of the household, and king; Odysseus contrived to avoid that fate, though faced with 108 potential Aegisthuses. Historically and sociologically these tales simply mean that some kings had established such personal power and authority that no challenge was possible, that others were challenged unsuccessfully, and that still others learned that 'first among equals' was no position from which to look forward to a long life of blessings and comforts, Nor was a Trojan War necessary as the igniting spark, although obviously such an enforced absence could facilitate the mobilization of hostile forces.

The uncertainties of kingship may be pursued one step backward in the career of Odysseus. What about Laertes? He was an old man, indeed, but he was not senile. Why did he not sit on the throne of Ithaca? Nestor was at least as old — about seventy in the *Iliad* — and he not only ruled before and after the war but accompanied the hosts to Troy; and there, though his value to the army was only moral and psychological, he was a leading member of Agamemnon's council of elders. And then there was old Priam. In the great crisis actual leadership fell to his son Hector, but Priam was still king beyond dispute. After Achilles had become reconciled with Agamemnon and returned to the fray, Aeneas came forward to challenge him to single combat. Why? asked Achilles. 'Does your heart command you to do battle with me in the hope of being master of Priam's lordship over the horse-taming Trojans? But no, even though you slay me, Priam will not on that account place the prerogative in your hands; for he has sons and he is firm and not weak-minded' (xx 179-83).

Nor is there a hint that Odysseus had usurped his father's position; on the contrary, much of the final book of the poem is given over to a scene of love and devotion between father and son. Yet so far was the ex-king from authority that all the while the suitors were threatening to destroy the very substance of his son and grandson, Laertes could do no more than withdraw in isolation to his farm, there to grieve and lament. Nobles lived in the town, not on their estates. Laertes, however, 'no longer comes to the town, but far off in the fields suffers misery, with an old woman as attendant, who serves him meat and drink whenever weariness takes hold of his limbs as he drags along the high ground of his vineyard'.*

It is idle to guess the circumstances which brought Odysseus to the throne in place of Laertes. The statement must suffice that long before the days when he could only drag himself in his vineyard Laertes had proved unable to rule *iphi*, by might. And so, somehow, the rule passed to his son. In a sense, what modern kings have called the principle of legitimacy was thereby preserved, the same principle which Achilles enunciated for Aeneas, and which he defended for his father Peleus and himself among his Myrmidons. That was Achilles's first concern in Hades when Odysseus paid his call. 'Tell me of excellent Peleus, if you have heard anything.' Does he still hold his rightful place or has he been pushed aside 'because old age has him by hand and foot'? For 'I am no longer his aid beneath the rays of the sun', protecting our rule with my might (11.494-503).

In Ithaca not even the arrogant suitors, for all their open threats of violence, could altogether overlook the family claim to the throne. On the surface there is no good reason why they went on with the game for so many years. If force had been the only factor, Leocritus spoke truly when he said they outnumbered any possible opposition; indeed, there was no visible opposition. Yet not only did they refrain from murdering Laertes and Telemachus and seizing power (although they did plot at the last

* 1.189-93. Note must be taken that a far less pathetic description appears elsewhere in the *Odyssey*, especially in the last book, thought by some scholars to have been composed relatively late: 'the fine and well-tilled farm of Laertes.... There was his house, and around it ran many huts on every side, in which the trusty slaves ate and sat and slept, who worked at his pleasure' (24.205-10). It is in this book, too, that we have the only explicit reference to Laertes ever having been king.

minute to assassinate the latter), not only did they publicly and repeatedly concede Telemachus's claim to his *oikos*, but they placed the decision in the strangest place imaginable, in the hands of a woman. There was nothing about the woman Penelope, either in beauty or wisdom or spirit, that could have won her this unprecedented and unwanted right of decision as a purely personal triumph. Institutionally, furthermore, this was a solidly patriarchal society, in which even a Telemachus could bid his mother leave the banquet hall and retire to her proper, womanly tasks.*

As his father's heir Telemachus obviously had a measure of authority, and Athena pointed to one way out. 'As for your mother, if her heart is stirred up to be married, let her return to the palace of her father great in might. They will arrange the wedding feast and array the many gifts, all that should go with a beloved daughter' (1.275-8). At the assembly on the next day both Antinous and Eurymachus gave him the same advice, the latter in the very words Athena had used. But 'wise' Telemachus demurred. 'It is bad for me to repay a large amount to Icarius [Penelope's father], should I myself send my mother back' (2.132-3). The 'large amount' was the dowry, which had to be restored under such circumstances.

Early in the feast at which Odysseus suddenly revealed himself and slaughtered the suitors, Telemachus made a remark to one of them which again indicated his authority, but in a different direction. 'I do not hinder the marriage of my mother; instead, I bid her marry whom she wishes and I also [offer to] give countless gifts. I am ashamed to drive her from the palace, against her will, by a word of compulsion' (20.341-4). But if Telemachus had the right to order his mother about in the matter of her marriage, either by sending her back to her father or by compelling (or preventing) her choice from among the wooers, how are we to explain, as fact or as law, Athena's rushing to Sparta, where Telemachus was visiting Menelaus, and warning him to return at once? 'For her [Penelope's] father and brother', said the goddess, 'are now bidding her marry Eurymachus, for he

* 1.356-9; 21.350-3.

outdoes all the suitors in gifts and he has greatly increased his gifts of wooing' (15.16-18).*

It has been argued that behind the confusions there lay the understandable uncertainty whether Odysseus was dead or alive, whether Penelope was a widow or not. Or perhaps the Penelope situation had become so muddled in the long prehistory of the *Odyssey* that the actual social and legal situation is no longer recoverable. Some scholars have adopted the desperate solution of finding in the account a vestige of a mother-right system that allegedly prevailed among the Greeks centuries before. They see similar traces in Phaeacia, and indeed the poet uses some very strange language about Queen Arete, niece and consort of Alcinous the king, even to underscoring her 'good wits' and her skill in resolving quarrels among men (7.73-4). When you enter the palace, Nausicaa advised Odysseus, pass by my father's throne and go directly to my mother and appeal to her. 'If she should be kindly disposed to you in her heart, then there is hope that you will see your friends, and come to your home good to dwell in, and to your native land.'† Both Arete and Alcinous were kindly disposed, it turned out, and Odysseus was welcomed beyond measure. After he had related many of his adventures, the queen, who was a full participant in the feasting, contrary to all the rules of Greek society of the time, called upon the nobles to supply gifts of treasure. 'He is my guest-friend, though each of you shares in the honour' (11.338). Not even Clytaemnestra would have talked that way, though she was not beyond joining in the plot to murder Agamemnon her lord.

However, one old Phaeacian noble promptly told Arete that, though her proposal was sound, 'on Alcinous here depend deed and word' (11.346). Nausicaa, too, before she counselled Odys-

---

* For the benefit of those who see in the coexistence of dowries and 'gifts of wooing' a sign of poetic imagination, on the argument that such 'opposite' practices are impossible in 'real life', it is perhaps worth calling attention to the shift that has been taking place in Greek Cypriot villages since 1930 in the system of marital property transfer. Opposing practices with respect to the provision of a house for newlyweds coexist there today, after nearly half a century of transition: see P. Loizos in *Man*, 10 (1975), pp. 503-23.

† 6.313-5; repeated by Athena, 7.75-7.

seus to seek out Arete, identified herself as the 'daughter of great-hearted Alcinous, on whom depend the force and the might of the Phaeacians' (16.196-7). And throughout the very long Phaeacian section of the poem Alcinous repeatedly exercised unmistakable and unchallenged royal authority. There are other difficulties and apparent contradictions in Phaeacia, not surprising in view of its position halfway between the world of fantasy Odysseus was finally leaving and the real world to which he was about to return. That a repressed memory of ancient matriarchy is reflected in some of the verses seems a singularly fragile argument. Neither Arete nor Penelope met the genealogical requirements of a matrilineal kinship structure, let alone of matriarchy: Arete was the daughter of Alcinous's elder brother; Penelope and Odysseus had no blood kinship at all.*

Whatever the explanation for Penelope's sudden acquisition of so puzzling a power of decision, in the end the essential fact is that 'as many of the nobles as have power in the islands, in Dulichion and Same and wooded Zacynthus, and as many as are lords in rocky Ithaca'† —in short, virtually the whole aristocracy in and around Ithaca —were agreed that the house of Odysseus was to be dethroned. Along with the rule, his successor was also to take his wife, his widow as many thought. On this point they were terribly insistent, and it may be suggested that their reasoning was this: that by Penelope's receiving the suitor of her choice into the bed of Odysseus, some shadow of legitimacy, however dim and fictitious, would be thrown over the new king. In his first speech to the assembly Telemachus had said that the wooers 'shrink from going to the house of her father Icarius, so that he might marry off his daughter and give her to whomsoever he chooses' (2.52-4). Icarius, would, of course, have chosen the highest bidder, the one who gave the most valuable gifts of wooing. Yet the suitors' unwillingness to follow this accepted procedure was surely more than niggardliness. If Icarius were to select Penelope's next husband, the successful bidder would ac-

* Among the matriarchal Iroquois, for example, the successor to a deceased chieftain was chosen by the matron of his maternal family.

† 1.245-7; repeated 16.122-4, with variations, 19.130-2.

quire a wife but not the kingdom. Rule in Ithaca was not for Icarius, an outsider, to bestow. That prerogative mysteriously belonged to Penelope.

And Penelope was their undoing. On instruction from Athena, she tricked the suitors into letting the returned hero, still in his beggarly disguise, get the great bow into his hands, which none but he could wield, and with it, supported by Telemachus and two slaves, Philoetius and Eumaeus, he slew the interlopers. Once again the narrative detail points to an essential element of Odyssean life: to regain his throne the king could count on no one but his wife, his son and his faithful slaves; in other words, royal power was personal power. Nothing could be more misleading than the analogy of king against barons at the close of the Middle Ages, in which the ultimate triumph of the royal principle rested on the backing of commoners. In war the commoners of Ithaca or Sparta or Argos took up arms; then, in the face of the hostile outsider (and especially of an invading outsider), the community was real and meaningful, and the king, as its head and representative, received support and obedience. In peace he was entitled to various perquisites, and under ordinary circumstances they were given freely. But when the lords fell out among themselves the issue was usually one for themselves alone.

Despite the general silence of the poems on the doings of the ordinary people of Greece, there is direct evidence on this score. Towards the close of the assembly summoned by Telemachus, Mentor complained: 'Now, indeed, I am angry with the rest of the people (*demos*), as you all sit in silence and do not upbraid the suitors and keep them in check, they being few and you many' (2.239-41). At the end of the tale, when the suitors were dead and Odysseus and his father were having their little feast of reunion at the old man's farm, there was another gathering in the *agora*. This was the meeting of the irate relatives of the victims, demanding blood vengeance. But it was no formal assembly. The men came together because 'Rumour the messenger went about the city' with the news of the slaughter (24.413) — Rumour, who was Zeus's messenger but had never been designated a herald in Ithaca. The poet makes it clear that this was a meeting of aristocrats (if there were commoners present, they came as retainers of noble households, not as members of the community of Ithaca). Hence here he never uses such words as *demos* or 'multitude', although some translators have mistakenly injected 'the people' into the lines.

The blood-feud rally was normal. Odysseus had himself anticipated such an action when he said to Telemachus after the slaughter of the suitors: 'Let us consider, that all may be for the very best. For a person who kills but one man in a country — even one for whom there are not many left behind to help — flees, forsaking his kinsmen and his fatherland. And we have killed the pillars of the city, the very noblest of the youths in Ithaca' (23.117-22). This was private vengeance. But what was the point, at the beginning of the poem, in calling an assembly to consider what Telemachus explicitly labelled a private matter? Throughout that meeting Telemachus never once addressed the people. He talked to the suitors, repeating in public what he had already demanded of them in private, that they give up their improper method of wooing. Only at the end did Mentor turn to the *demos* and say: I am angry with you that you do not intervene. Telemachus had clearly failed in his purpose, which was to try to mobilize public opinion against the suitors, thus transforming a private matter into a public one, in effect. Realizing this, Mentor brought the issue into the open, again without success. That is why Leocritus could answer with a sneer, 'It is difficult to fight against greater numbers about a feast' (2.244-5). Mentor had stressed the potential power of the *demos*: 'they [the suitors] being few and you many'. Oh no, replied Leocritus, the many are disinterested and neutral, and therefore we and our kinsmen and retainers outnumber you and the forces you can muster. Odysseus himself would 'meet with evil destiny, were he to fight against greater numbers' (2.250-1).

Neutrality is a state of mind, and anyone who enters the arena to fight for power must keep his eyes and ears on the audience; their attitude may shift suddenly, and they may swarm into the pit and take sides. After the plan to ambush Telemachus had failed, Antinous argued with the other suitors that further delay was perilous. Let us take him into the fields, Antinous proposed, and do away with him, for 'the multitude no longer bear good will to us in all respects. Come, therefore, before he calls the Achaeans together to an assembly' and tells them how we plotted against his life. 'Hearing of these evil deeds, they will not approve. Beware, then, lest they do us evil and drive us from our land, and we come to the country of others' (16.375-82).

Antinous feared that the *demos*, previously unmoved by Telemachus's appeal, might now decide to take sides. Notably there was no reference to rights in his speech. It was not the assertion of popular rights that he foresaw, but Telemachus's rapid coming of age, his beginning to rule by might, and hence the danger that he could persuade the *demos* out of its neutrality and into direct action. Perhaps the memory was still with Antinous of the day when his father had fled to Odysseus for asylum from the *demos*, 'for they were terribly angry because he had gone off with the Taphian pirates to raid the Thesprotians, who were in friendly relations with us' (16.425-7).

Hypothetically, at least, the opposite possibility was also conceivable — that the people would shift to the position of the suitors. When Telemachus was Nestor's guest, Nestor asked him point blank why he continued to suffer the suitors. 'Tell me, do you yield willingly or do the people hate you up and down the land, obeying the voice of a god?' (3.214-5). Telemachus made no direct reply then, but he was asked the identical question on another occasion, this time by Odysseus in beggarly disguise (16.95-6), and he said that the answer was no to both alternatives. Lack of power alone caused his passivity.

In fact, we are never told what the *demos* of Ithaca really thought about the whole affair. The narrative reached its end without their intervention on either side, despite all the questioning, the doubts and the fears, the efforts to influence public opinion. Like Eliot's women of Canterbury, the *demos* of Ithaca seemed to say by its neutrality:

> *King rules or barons rule; . . .*
> *But mostly we are left to our own devices,*
> *And we are content if we are left alone.*

The suitors failed to take up Antinous's proposal that they seek a solution by murdering Telemachus. Whether his fears were warranted or not is unanswerable, for another ending was already prepared. While the conference was going on, Odysseus was hiding in Ithaca, and the suitors were soon to meet death at his hands. What, we may speculate, would have happened had a chance arrow brought Odysseus down at that moment? It does not necessarily follow that the *demos* would have been moved to reprisal. Nothing in the accepted rules of behaviour, neither divine precept nor convention, demanded that they act. Homicide was no crime in a public sense, and regicide was but a special kind of homicide. Had Odysseus been killed, Telemachus would have faced a choice: he could play Hamlet or he could play Orestes. That was his familial responsibility; the community had none. 'And of the son of Atreus even you have heard, though far off,' Nestor had said to Telemachus; 'how he came and how Aegisthus devised his evil end. But sadly indeed did he pay for it. How good it is that a son of the man should be left, as that son took vengeance on wily Aegisthus, his father's murderer' (3.193-8). Telemachus's misfortune was that, faced not with a single enemy but with 108, he came from a line of only sons and had no blood-brothers upon whom to call.

Blood vengeance is but the most dramatic indicator that in the world of Odysseus personal power meant the strength of the household and the family. In that sense the personalization of kingly power went very deep. The suitors may have denied any hostile intentions against the *oikos* of Odysseus, but this was an atypical situation in every respect, and Antinous finally suggested that they kill Telemachus and divide the estate among themselves. The rule was complete identity between king's treasury and king's *oikos*, precisely as his personal retainers were his public officials. The gold and bronze and grain and wine and fine cloth that Telemachus saw lying in the locked storeroom belonged to his father and would come to him by inheritance, whether they had been acquired by Odysseus as king or by Odysseus as mere nobleman. No wonder Telemachus said with charmingly naïve pathos, when it seemed that the suitors must surely triumph, 'For indeed it is no bad thing to be a king: forthwith his house becomes wealthy and he himself most honoured' (1.392-3).

The base of royal wealth and power lay in the holdings in land and cattle, without which no man could have become king in the first place. While the king reigned he also had the use of a separate estate, called a *temenos*, which the community placed at his disposal.* This was the sole exception to the rule that all royal possessions and acquisitions melted into his private *oikos*.

Next on the list of 'royal revenues' came booty—an all-embracing word covering cattle, metal, female captives, and whatever else of wealth was seizable (except land, for the simple reason that wars were not fought for territory and did not lead to its acquisition). In his guise as a Cretan beggar Odysseus boasted to Eumaeus of his former glory. 'Nine times did I lead men and fleet ships against men of another land, and very much [booty] fell to me, of which I chose what suited me, and much I then obtained by lot' (14.230-3). The ruler thus not only shared with his men in the general distribution of the spoils, equalized by the drawing of lots, but he received an added share, by first choice. In a major expedition the commander-in-chief took the royal share, though other kings were among his followers. 'My hands bear the brunt of furious battle; but when the distribution comes your prerogatives are far greater, and I go to my ships bearing something slight, but dear to me, when I am weary of fighting' (1 165-8). So Achilles to Agamemnon, and though 'something slight' underrates the acquisitions of the 'sacker of cities',† there is no mistaking the measure of his resentment against Agamemnon, his inferior in prowess but his superior, by right of position, in the sharing of the fruits.

And then there were the gifts, endlessly given and endlessly talked about. No word immediately denoting compulsion, like

---

* The same word was applied to a temple estate set aside for the enjoyment of a god. With the decay of kingship in post-Homeric Greece, the latter became the sole meaning of *temenos*.

† 'Something slight, but dear to me' appears twice in the *Odyssey*, in a begging context (6.208; 14.58).

'taxes' or even feudal 'dues', is to be found in the poems for payments from people to ruler, apart from the context of the special prerogative in the distribution of booty and of the meat of sacrificial animals. 'And seven well situated cities will I give him . . .,' said Agamemnon. 'And there dwell men of many flocks and many herds, who will honour him like a god with gifts.'* Details of this gift-giving by the people are utterly lacking; for Ithaca it is not even mentioned. That it took its place, however, alongside booty as an important and continuing reason why it was 'no bad thing to be a king' can scarcely be doubted.

At times the gifts, like the benevolences of Charles I, seem something less than voluntary. 'Come now,' said King Alcinous of the Phaeacians to the nobles feasting the parting of Odysseus, 'let us each give him a great tripod and a cauldron; and we in turn shall gather among the people and be recompensed, for it is burdensome for one person to give without recompense' (13.13-15). Nevertheless, it would be a false appreciation to see nothing but euphemism in the insistence on calling such payments 'gifts'. For one thing, they lacked the regularity of taxes or dues as well as their fixity of amount. Even so limited a play of free choice as the time and amount of the payment gave it overtones of sentiment and value ordinarily absent from taxation. It is difficult to measure this psychological distinction, but it cannot be ignored for that reason. 'Honour him like a god with gifts.' Fear the gods as one may, they are not tax collectors, and man's relationship to them is of another order. In the same way, a gift to a ruler, even when compulsory for all practical purposes, is in its formal voluntarism of another order from the fixed tax with its openly coercive character.

What was the counter-gift to the people? The answer is chiefly in the area we label foreign affairs. The effective, powerful king gave protection and defence, by his dealings with kings abroad, by his organization of such activities as the building of walls,

* IX 149-55. Agamemnon's long descriptions of his proposed gift of amends to Achilles is repeated to Achilles by Odysseus, word for word, IX 264-98; the passage quoted here is found in lines 291-7. Agamemnon's right of disposal over seven cities is a unique and unexplained instance in the poems.

and by his personal leadership in battle. He was 'shepherd of the people', a Homeric commonplace that had none of the Arcadian image in it, only Goethe's 'he who is no warrior can be no shepherd'.* Sarpedon, commander of the Lycian contingent supporting the Trojans, made the point bluntly: 'Glaucus, why are we two the most honoured in Lycia in seats of honour and meat and full goblets, and all look upon us as gods, and we hold a great *temenos* on the banks of the Xanthus, a fine one of orchard-land and wheat-bearing land? Therefore we must now stand in the first ranks of the Lycians and participate in fiery battle, so that some of the Lycians armed with stout cuirasses may say, "Our kings who are lords in Lycia are indeed not inglorious, they that eat fat sheep and choice honey-sweet wine; oh no, they are also of stout might, since they fight in the first ranks of the Lycians"' (XII 310-21).

The king gave military leadership and protection, and he gave little else, despite some hints of royal justice (and injustice) scattered through the *Odyssey*, once in a lengthier green-pastures simile: 'O lady [Penelope], no one among mortal men throughout the boundless earth would blame you, for your fame reaches the wide heaven, as does [the fame] of an excellent king, one who, god-fearing and ruling among men many and mighty, upholds righteousness, and the dark earth bears wheat and barley and the trees are heavy with fruit, and the flocks bear without fail, and the sea gives forth fish, out of [his] good leadership, and the people thrive under him' (19.107-14). This direct linking of right rule and the fruitfulness of nature is anachronistic, as is the notion of 'god-fearing'; they belong not to the time of Odysseus but to the eighth or seventh century B.C., when the idea of a world ordered by divine justice had entered men's minds. They belong in the poems of Hesiod, not in the *Odyssey*. Everything that Homer tells us demonstrates that here he permitted a contemporary note to enter, carefully restricting it, however, to a harmless simile and thus avoiding any possible contradiction in the narrative itself. The return of Odysseus to the throne of Ithaca was just and

* Quoted from H. Fränkel, *Die homerischen Gleichnisse* (Göttingen: Vandenhoeck, 1921), p. 60.

proper, but it was a matter of private action for personal interests, not the triumph of righteousness in the public interest.

One need scarcely ask why Alcinous did not let the people make a direct gift to Odysseus. Tripods and cauldrons were treasure, things which only the aristocracy possessed in significant quantity. Nor would it have been fitting for the common people to provide the gifts to speed a hero on his journey. In a society so status-bound, in which gift-giving had a quantity of ceremonialism about it, no one could just give a gift to anyone else. There were rather strict lines of giving, and grades and ranks of objects. Stated in other terms, the gift and the relationship between giver and recipient were inseparable. What went up the line from the people to their lord was one matter; what went to an outsider was something else again, and no confusion between the two was permissible.

However the psychologists understand the affective side of this gift-giving, functionally it took its place with marriage and with armed might as an act through which status relations were created, and what we should call political obligations. The world of Odysseus was split into many communities more or less like Ithaca. Among them, between each community and every other one, the normal relationship was one of hostility, at times passive, in a kind of armed truce, and at times active and bellicose. When the slaughtered suitors entered Hades, the arrival *en masse* of the 'best men' of Ithaca was startling, and automatically it was attributed to one of two causes. 'Did Poseidon', asked the shade of Agamemnon, 'stir up heavy winds and high waves and overpower you in your ships? Or did hostile men slay you on dry land while you were rustling cattle and fair flocks of sheep, or while they were defending their city and their women?'*

In so permanently hostile an environment the heroes were permitted to seek allies; their code of honour did not demand that they stand alone against the world. But there was nothing in their social system that created the possibility for two communities, as such, to enter an alliance. Only personal devices were avail-

* 24.109-13. In the earlier scene in Hades, Odysseus greeted the shade of Agamemnon with the identical words (11.399-403).

able, through the channels of household and kin. The first of these was marriage, which served, among other things, to establish new lines of kin, and hence of mutual obligation, that crossed and criss-crossed the Hellenic world. Only men arranged marriages, and only a man from whom Zeus had taken his wits would have neglected considerations of wealth, power, and support in making his selection.

Several generations of such calculated dealing out of daughters and assorted female relatives created an intricate, and sometimes confusing, network of obligations. That was one reason why the heroes memorized their genealogies carefully and recited them often. When Diomedes and Glaucus 'came together in the middle between the two [armies], eager to do battle', the former stopped and asked a question. 'Who are you, brave sir, of mortal men? For never before have I seen you in glorious battle.' Glaucus's reply was a long recital, full sixty-five lines, chiefly of the heroic exploits and the begettings of his grandfather Bellerophon. His final words were: 'Of this lineage and blood I vaunt myself to be.'

'So said he,' the poet went on, 'and Diomedes of the brave war-cry rejoiced. . . . "In truth, you are my paternal guest-friend of old; for illustrious Oineus at one time entertained excellent Bellerophon in his palace and for twenty days he kept him, and they gave each other fine gifts of guest-friendship. . . . Therefore I am now a dear guest-friend to you in central Argos, and you [to me] in Lycia whenever I come to your land. So let us avoid each other's spears"' — there are Trojans enough for me to kill, and Greeks for you. '"Let us exchange armour with each other, so that they too may know that we avow ourselves to be paternal guest-friends."' *

This is not comedy. Homer was no Shaw, Diomedes no chocolate-cream soldier. Guest-friendship was a very serious institution, the alternative to marriage in forging bonds between rulers; and there could have been no more dramatic test of its value in holding the network of relationships together than just such a critical

* VI 119-231. That was the occasion when Glaucus went witless and gave golden armour for bronze.

moment. Guest-friend and guest-friendship were far more than sentimental terms of human affection. In the world of Odysseus they were technical names for very concrete relationships, as formal and as evocative of rights and duties as marriage. And they remained so well thereafter: Herodotus (1.69) tells how, in the middle of the sixth century before Christ, Croesus, king of Lydia, 'sent messengers to Sparta bearing gifts and requesting an alliance'. The Spartans 'rejoiced at the coming of the Lydians and they took the oaths of guest-friendship and alliance'.

The Herodotus story documents the persistence of guest-friendship; it also shows how far the Greek world had moved from the days of Odysseus. Croesus exchanged oaths of guest-friendship with the Spartans, but Homer knew of no such tie between Argives and Lycians or Taphians and Ithacans — only between individuals, Diomedes and Glaucus, 'Mentes' and Telemachus. 'Guest-friend', it is understood, is the conventional, admittedly clumsy, English rendition of the Greek *xenos* in one of its senses. The same Greek word also meant 'stranger', 'foreigner', and sometimes 'host', a semantic range symbolic of the ambivalence which characterized all dealings with the stranger in that archaic world.

The first thing we are told about the Phaeacians — immediately establishing the Utopianism of the tale — is that they existed in almost complete isolation; in fact, that Alcinous's father, Nausithous, had transplanted the community from Hypereia to Scheria (both mythical places) to that very end. There is no cause to fear, Nausicaa reassured her maids as they ran from Odysseus on the beach. 'That mortal man does not exist, neither has he been born, who comes to the land of the Phaeacians bringing war, for we are very dear to the immortals. We live far off, surrounded by the stormy sea, the outermost of men, and no other mortals have dealing with us' (6.201-5). Nausicaa overstated the situation a little. After she had escorted Odysseus to the town, Athena took over and threw a covering of mist about him to ensure his safe arrival at the palace. 'Neither look at any man', was the goddess's warning, 'nor inquire of one. For they do not readily bear with strangers' (7.31-2).

That was one pole: fear, suspicion, distrust of the stranger. With it went his rightlessness, his lack of kin to safeguard or avenge him, as the case may have been, against ill-doing. At the other pole was the general human obligation of hospitality: in one of his attributes the father of the immortals was Zeus Xenios, the god of hospitality. It was precisely in Phaeacia that, after the earlier forebodings, Odysseus was welcomed so richly that King Alcinous and his court became proverbial among later Greeks for their luxurious living. That paradox was a model of the basic ambivalence of the heroic world toward the uninvited stranger, of the rapid oscillation between deep, well-warranted fear and lavish entertainment.

The poet underscores his point in another way among the Cyclopes, in pure Never-Never Land. Odysseus's opening gambit was to plead for the traditional hospitality, and Polyphemus replied with the most open cynicism: I shall devour you last among your company; 'that shall be my gift of hospitality' (9.370). Polyphemus stood at one pole only; there was nothing confusing or uncertain about his unmitigated hostility to all strangers. And again Homer had caught the right shading. We, said the Cyclops, 'give no heed to aegis-bearing Zeus, nor to the blessed gods, inasmuch as we are far better' (9.275-6). The giant was to pay for his *hybris* soon enough, tricked by the superior craftiness of god-fearing Odysseus. Behind the fairy-tale, clearly, there lay a distinct view of social evolution. In primitive times, the poet seems to be suggesting, man lived in a state of permanent struggle and war to the death against the outsider. Then the gods intervened, and through their precepts, their *themis*, a new ideal was set before man, and especially before a king, an obligation of hospitality: 'all strangers and beggars are from Zeus' (14.57-8). Henceforth men had to pick a difficult path between the two, between the reality of a society in which the stranger was still a problem and a threat, and the newer morality, according to which he was somehow covered by the aegis of Zeus.

Institutionally it was guest-friendship above all that weakened the tension between the poles. Trade may have removed the enmity from the surface for a moment, but it made no lasting contribution in this area. On the contrary, trade tended to strengthen suspicion of the outsider, for all its indispensability. The unrelieved, totally negative Homeric image of the Phoenicians makes that absolutely clear. Once again the point is driven home in Utopia. The Phaeacians were the ideal seamen, men who, unlike the Greeks themselves, had no horror of the sea and no reason to dread it. 'For the Phaeacians have no pilots and no rudders, which other ships have; but [the ships] themselves understand the thoughts and intents of men' (8.557-9). Yet not only is there no single reference to Phaeacian trade, but it was in Phaeacia that Odysseus received the crowning insult of being likened to a merchant.

Guest-friendship was of an altogether different order and conception. The stranger who had a *xenos* in a foreign land — and every other community was foreign soil — had an effective substitute for kinsmen, a protector, representative and ally. He had a refuge if he were forced to flee his home, a storehouse on which to draw when compelled to travel, and a source of men and arms if drawn into battle. These were all personal relations, but with the powerful lords the personal merged into the political, and then guest-friendship was the Homeric version, or forerunner, of political and military alliances. Not that every guest-friend automatically and invariably responded to a call to arms; that would have been a pattern of uniformity unattained, and unattainable, in the fluid and unstable political situation of the world of Odysseus. In this respect a guest-friend was like a king; his worth was in direct proportion to his power. During the years of his unexplained absence, all of Odysseus's *xenoi* might well have agreed with his father Laertes when he said to one, 'the countless gifts which you gave, you bestowed in vain' (24.283).

As the suitors entered Hades, Agamemnon's shade addressed Amphimedon in particular. 'Do you not remember the time when I came to your house there [in Ithaca] with godlike Menelaus, to urge Odysseus to go along with me to Ilion in the well-benched ships? And it was a whole month before we had sailed across the wide sea, for it was with difficulty that we prevailed upon Odysseus sacker of cities.'* To recruit an army among outsiders in what was, to begin with, only a family feud over a stolen wife, Agamemnon naturally made the fullest use of his guest-friends. But having called upon Amphimedon for the service of hospitality, Agamemnon apparently did not ask for his military services. For that he went to Odysseus, the king, with whom he had no formal relationship.

It would be an idle game to try to guess why Amphimedon stayed at home. Or why Odysseus, having finally been prevailed upon and having raised an army, did not, or could not, engage a larger proportion of the Ithacan nobility in the expedition. The fact is that we are left in rather complete darkness about the way the Achaean army was put together. Perhaps the procedure in Ithaca was the same as among Achilles's Myrmidons. There one son from each family was chosen by lot (XXIV 397-400). More likely the methods varied from community to community, according to the desires, interests, and, above all, powers of the respective kings and nobles. No Greek community had been attacked or even threatened; hence participation in the Trojan War was of no direct concern to the *demos*.

Again we are reminded of the fluidity of the political scene. Agamemnon, the most powerful of the many rulers among the Hellenes, had as his guest-friend in Ithaca not the king, Odysseus, but one of the non-ruling aristocrats, Amphimedon. There was nothing strange or rare about this. It was repeated all over the Greek world, just as marriage, rigidly bound within class lines, was perfecly acceptable between king or king's son and the daughter of a noble who was not a king. 'First among equals' meant equality of status with respect to the two peaceful relationships that could be established across community lines, marriage and guest-friendship. There could be no notion of blood royal in a world in which 'there are many other kings' in each community.

A third kind of relationship existed, however, in which inequality was expressed — that of the retainer. While marriage

* 24.115-19. Presumably it was to Amphimedon's father, Melaneus, that Agamemnon came, for Amphimedon would have been a child then. In what follows I continue to refer to Amphimedon for convenience.

and guest-friendship went outside the community—the latter always, the former sometimes—retainership was a strictly internal institution, one that set up a loose hierarchy among the nobles of a community and played a key role in the internal power structure. The situation may be stated in another way: the retainers constituted the third essential element of the aristocratic household, the other two being the members of the family and the labour force (whether slaves or hirelings). 'Retainer' is a loose word, and that is why it fits the Greek *therapon*. At one end of the scale it defines the free but surely not aristocratic attendants at the palace banquets, who performed the offices 'whereby inferiors serve their betters' (15.324). And at the other end is a hero like Meriones, *therapon* of King Idomeneus of Crete. Meriones enjoys some of the proudest epithets in the poems, such as 'the equal of fleet Ares' or 'leader of men' (XIII 295, 304); he is one of the very few secondary chieftains named in the catalogue of ships; and his battle prowess receives many lines in the *Iliad*. Nevertheless, it must be assumed that Meriones, as a *therapon*, followed Idomeneus to Troy as a matter of obligation, not because he had been 'prevailed upon'.

Obligations of this nature and intensity, like the obligations imposed by lineage, were personal. That does not mean that they were arbitrary, weak or uncertain, but it does mean that in very large measure they stood apart from and outside the bonds of community; or better, that they stood above. It was Menelaus who was aggrieved by the flight of Helen, not Sparta. It was his brother Agamemnon who assumed leadership of the war of reprisal, not Mycenae. It was Amphimedon and Odysseus to whom Agamemnon appealed for assistance, not Ithaca. But it was all of Troy that fought back, not out of loyalty to Paris—or even to old Priam, who was bound to uphold his son—but because the Greek invaders threatened to destroy them all.

The ceaseless interplay of household, kin and community, at home and abroad, created a complex variety of individual situations and difficulties. Yet there was a kind of fundamental pattern and a trend which, though not really discernible in the poems themselves, can be seen through that most useful of all the instruments of the historian, hindsight. The anthropologists have taught us what a kinship society looks like in its purer forms. It is characteristic of much of the primitive world that 'the conduct of individuals to one another is very largely regulated on the basis of kinship, this being brought about by the formation of fixed patterns of behaviour for each recognized kind of kinship relation.'* This is no description of the world of Odysseus, in which the family tie, though strong, was narrowly defined, and in which other strong and often more binding relationships were established outside the blood group. In evolutionary terms, in so far as they may legitimately be employed, the world of the Homeric poems had advanced beyond the primitive. Kinship was then but one of several organizing principles, and not the most powerful one. Pre-eminence lay in the *oikos*, the large noble household with its staff of slaves and commoners, its aristocratic retainers, and its allies among relatives and guest-friends.

Within the household, as within a lineage, the behaviour patterns of man to man (and to woman) were graded and fixed. As between households, too, there were many customary rules of what was proper and what was not, and we must believe that in the daily routine of life they were obeyed as a matter of course. But a higher coercive power was largely lacking, the community principle being still so rudimentary. Therefore, as one princely *oikos* vied with another for greater wealth and power, for more prestige and a superior status, breaches of the rules were common enough to create the almost unbroken tension that was the stamp of heroic existence. In time to come great moral teachers would make much of this conflict between status, prestige, and power on the one side and divine *themis* on the other. Neither the heroes nor their minstrels were systematic thinkers. Moral principles and philosophical abstractions were no doubt inherent in their tales, but the bards were content simply to tell the story.

'It is no bad thing to be a king', said one of the characters in the story. Yet one need only turn the pages of Homer or read at random in the legends of the Greeks to discover that betrayal

* A. R. Radcliffe-Brown, *Structure and Function in Primitive Society* (London: Cohen and West, 1952), p. 29.

and assassination were a most common fate among rulers. Olympian Zeus himself had become chief of the gods only by overthrowing his father Cronus and the other Titans, and Cronus before him found the path to power equally bloody. One may assess the meaning of the myth-symbols as one wishes. One may allow for the fact that narrative poetry is poetry of action, and that before the invention of romantic love, deeds of violence made up the whole of the thematic material. Nevertheless, it is scarcely conceivable that the tales could have remained so one-sided in their murders, rapes, seductions, fratricides, patricides, and plottings had kingship in reality been a comfortable position of perquisites in a regular dynastic succession.

Nor was this merely a matter of open conflict over who should hold the throne. Behind that there emerged a more fundamental and, in the end, decisive issue. In promoting his own and his household's interests, the king-aristocrat became the agent of the community principle: the stronger the sense of community and the broader its powers, the greater the king and the more secure in his position. In reply, the aristocracy demanded hegemony for the *oikos* and for their class, under a king if possible, without a king if need be. Homer records many incidents in this conflict and he makes no secret of his own preference for kingly rule, notably in his idealization of royal rule among the Phaeacians. He gives no clues to the outcome, but we know it well. By the time the *Odyssey* was written the defeat of the kings had been so complete that kingship was gone from most of Hellas. In its place the aristocrats ruled as a group, equals without a first among them.

And then the aristocrats found themselves with a new menace, undreamed of in the world of Odysseus. The *demos*, nearly always a passive bystander in the earlier political conflicts, began to know its own strength and capacity for rule. In the *Iliad* and the *Odyssey* it grumbled or it acclaimed but it took orders. That was the recognized role of inferiors, to 'honour him like a god'. On one occasion Agamemnon tried to use psychology on his troops, with such ill success that panic set in and the whole Greek army, become a mob, began to embark in disorder, determined to sail for home and abandon the war. Hera intervened and sent Athena to Odysseus with instructions that he pull himself together and put a stop to the disgraceful flight. Taking Agamemnon's sceptre, Odysseus went among the solidiers, cajoling and árguing as he moved.

'When he came to one who was a king and a man of eminence, he stood beside him and restrained him with gentle words. . . . But whatever man of the *demos* [i.e. commoner] he saw and found him shouting, him he struck with the sceptre, upbraiding him in these words: "Good sir, sit still and hearken to the words of those who are your betters, you who are no warrior and a weakling, who are not counted either in battle or in council"' (II 188-202).

That principle remained unchallenged in Odysseus's day. Whatever the conflicts and cleavages among the noble households and families, they were always in accord that there could be no crossing of the great line which separated the *aristoi* from the many, the heroes from the non-heroes.

Chapter 5

MORALS AND VALUES

Much of the twenty-third book of the *Iliad* is given over to an account of the funeral games staged by Achilles in honour of Patroclus. Before the assembled Achaean host the best athletes among the heroes competed in what later became standard Greek events, the chariot race, the foot race, boxing, wrestling, and also in weight throwing. 'And from his ships Achilles brought out prizes, cauldrons and tripods and horses and mules and strong oxen, and also well-girdled women and gray iron' (XXIII 259-61). The first event, described with fantastic power, brilliance and precision, was the chariot race won by Diomedes. Nestor's son Antilochus barely defeated Menelaus for second place, but only because he had fouled the Spartan king on the far turn. Fourth came Meriones, and far to the rear poor Eumelus, thrown from his chariot when the yoke cracked, and forced to complete the course on foot, pulling the chariot behind him.

There was a prize for each competitor, in a sequence specified by Achilles beforehand. Diomedes immediately took the slave woman and tripod designated for the victor. Then Achilles proposed — remarkably, it must be said — that Eumelus be given the second prize, a mare, as a mark of compassion for his sorry luck, and the audience assented by acclamation, precisely as if they were sitting in formal assembly. Whereupon Antilochus 'rose and spoke of his right. "O Achilles, I shall be exceedingly angry with you if you carry out what you have said."' As for Eumelus, '"he ought to have prayed to the immortals, then he would not have come in last of all in the race. If you have pity on him, and he is dear to your heart, you have much gold in your hut, you have copper and sheep, you have slave women and uncloven horses. Take from these and give him an even greater prize. . . . But this one I will not give. For her, let him who will try battle at my hand."' Achilles smiled and conceded.

'But Menelaus also rose among them, sore at heart, full of indignation at Antilochus. A herald placed the sceptre in his hand and bade the Argives be silent. And then the godlike [*isotheos*, literally "god-equal"] man addressed them: "Antilochus, you had been wise before, what kind of behaviour was this? You dishonoured my valour and you interfered with my horses, pushing ahead yours, which are very inferior. But come, chieftains and leaders of the Argives, state the right between the two of us."'

Before the chieftains and leaders could state the right, however, Menelaus changed his mind and adopted an alternative procedure. '"Come now, I myself will state the right, and I believe that none of the Danaans will rebuke me, for it will be straight. Antilochus, come here, fosterling of Zeus. According to proper procedure (*themis*), stand before your horses and chariot, take in your hand the thin whip with which you drove before, and, with your hand on the horses, swear by [Poseidon] the earth-mover and earth-shaker that you did not deliberately interfere with my chariot by a trick."' But Nestor's son, 'who had been wise' until his eagerness to win impelled him to trickery, had recovered his wisdom by then, enough to refuse this challenge to perjure himself in the name of Poseidon. He apologized, offered the mare to Menelaus, and restored the peace.

Homer gave this scene the outward form of a regular *agora*, which it unquestionably was not. Nor did it have to be. Menelaus demanded his right and he had the choice of methods, neither of which required an assembly. The issue between him and Antilochus could either be submitted to arbitration, as he first proposed, or it could be decided by oath. The two procedures were equal in validity and fully interchangeable; they were both ways of 'stating the right', and they were both final, without appeal to any higher earthly authority. Should the answer turn out to be crooked, rather than straight, then the gods would have to arrange proper punishment. Had Antilochus, for example, accepted the challenge and perjured himself, beyond a doubt Poseidon would have taken merciless vengeance for so great an insult to his honour. But it was not the business of any mortal to raise the charge of false swearing.

The earlier issue of right was between Antilochus and Eumelus. Antilochus chose a third method, trial by armed combat. And the decision thus arrived at, had anyone taken him up, would also have been final: to the victor goes the right. There is a nice touch here, though an irrelevant one: between Antilochus and Eumelus there was no question of fact; Eumelus had finished last and Antilochus would have beaten him even if he had raced fairly. Nevertheless, Antilochus could have chosen arbitration or the oath, just as Menelaus could have made trial with Antilochus by the sword. With variations in detail, these were the three ways, and the only three ways, that were available to the Homeric heroes for the settlement of disputes over rights.

Apart from the moment when the people acclaimed Achilles's gesture of compassion for Eumelus, the assemblage, heroes and *demos* alike, remained passive spectators. The defence of a right was a purely private matter. He who felt aggrieved had the responsibility to take the necessary steps and the right to choose from among the available methods. His kin or his guest-friends, retainers and followers might intervene in support, but still as a private action. Although there are a few fragmentary phrases in the poems about royal judgements, they are contemporary notes, and therefore anachronistic, which slipped by the poet. He was composing at a time when the community principle had advanced to a point of some limited public administration of justice. But he was singing about a time when that was not the case, except for the intangible power of public opinion. How imposing a factor that was cannot be estimated, but it was surely significant and it must at times have led to intervention by outsiders to keep the peace. The principle remained, however, of strictly private rights privately protected. In no other way would the suitor theme of the *Odyssey* have been intelligible, and without the suitors' ruthless persistence and Telemachus's impotence there would have been no *Odyssey*.

Menelaus and Antilochus were equals in status. That was an essential fact, for justice among the heroes, like justice in the aristocratic code of honour of more modern times, was a matter for equals alone. Menelaus could no more have challenged Ther-

sites to an oath than a Prussian Junker could have challenged a
Berlin shopkeeper to a duel. Odysseus, we remember, stopped the
panic in the Greek forces by appealing gently to the captains
and by using the club and the command on the rank and file.
The poet was not satisfied to close the scene on that note; instead,
he took the opportunity to write a little essay on social classes and
the modes of behaviour proper to each. Once Odysseus had succeeded in returning the men to the *agora*, the narrative took a
new turn.

'Now all the others sat down and remained orderly in their
seats; only Thersites the loose-tongued kept on scolding, he
whose heart was full of words, many and disorderly, quarrelling
with the kings vainly and not in good order.... And he was the
ugliest man who came to Ilion. He was bandy-legged and lame
in one foot; his two shoulders were hunched and bent in upon
his chest, and above them his head was misshapen, with sparse
hair growing on it.' The substance of Thersites's complaint was
this: The devil with fighting to amass booty for Agamemnon; let
us go home.

Odysseus strode to Thersites, ordered him to cease from his
reviling of kings, and threatened to drive him naked and weeping
from the assembly. 'He spoke thus and beat him on the back and
shoulders with the sceptre. And he doubled up and a big tear
fell from him, and a bloody welt rose on his back beneath the
golden sceptre. Then he sat down and was frightened; smarting
with pain and looking foolish, he wiped away the tear. The others,
though they were sorry, laughed lightly at him, and this is how
one would speak, glancing at his neighbour: "Oh yes! In truth
Odysseus has done countless good things before, being pre-
eminent in sound counsels and marshalling battles, but this is by
far the best thing he has done among the Argives, that he has
stopped this foul-mouthed slanderer from haranguing. Hardly, I
think, will his arrogant heart again bid him rail at kings with
words of reproach." So spoke the multitude' (II 211-78).

Those final words, 'so spoke the multitude', protest too much.
It is as if the poet himself felt that he had overdrawn the contrast.
Do not think I talk from an aristocratic bias—that is the sense of

the last four words. Even the commoners among the Hellenes stood aghast at Thersites's defective sense of fitness, and, though they pitied him as one of their own, they concurred with full heart in the rebuke administered by Odysseus and in the methods he employed. 'This is by far the best thing he has done among the Argives' indeed, for Thersites had gnawed at the foundations on which the world of Odysseus was erected.

Of course, Homer reflected the views and values of the aristocracy, from the opening line of the *Iliad* to the final sentence of the *Odyssey*. But what does that tell us? Does it mean, for example, that he is never to be trusted when he puts an idea or sentiment on the tongue of a Thersites or a Eumaeus? To answer that question in the affirmative would be to imagine a society in which aristocrats and commoners held two completely contradictory sets of values and beliefs, a society such as the world has never known. Beyond a doubt there were two standards in certain spheres of behaviour, with respect to the ethos of work, for example, or in the protection of rights. Odysseus's employment of the sceptre offers a fine symbol. On this occasion he had the use of Agamemnon's sceptre, a gift from Zeus himself, fashioned by Hephaestus for the king of the gods, given by Zeus to Pelops, from whom it passed to Atreus, from Atreus to Thyestes, and then to Agamemnon, grandson of Pelops (it finally came to rest as a sacred relic in Plutarch's native city of Chaeronea). The sceptre, any sceptre, was not only the symbol of authority, it was also the mark of *themis*, of orderly procedure, and so it was given to each assembly speaker in turn to secure his inviolability, as when Menelaus rose to challenge Antilochus. Against Thersites, however, it was a club, for Thersites was of those 'who are not counted either in battle or in council'. He harangued the assembly without *themis*, he had been given no sceptre by the herald, therefore it was proper for him to receive it across the back.

The trouble is that we simply do not know how rights were determined when commoners were involved, whether between noble and commoner or between commoner and commoner. Neither Homer nor his audience cared about such matters and we have no other source of information. This unconcern goes much deeper, extending to virtually the whole of the value scale. We are left to guess, and with little to base our guesses on. The evidence of what has been called the peasant type of heroic poetry, oral epics composed and recited among peasants rather than in the halls of barons—a very widespread type in many regions of Europe and Asia—tends to argue that they often told the same kind of stories, about the same kinds of heroes, with the identical values and virtues, as the aristocratic epic of the Homeric type. Against that there is the bitterness of Hesiod, with his peasant orientation, as well as the strong inference that in matters of religion, at least, Homer's indifference to the common people entailed a deliberate rejection of popular religious beliefs and practices. Presumably the commoner of Ithaca stood somewhat in the middle, sharing many notions and sentiments with Odysseus, but giving others a different colouring. By and large it is a useless exercise to seek these shadings. What we have on a very rich canvas are the morals and values of a warrior culture, and with that we must be content.

'Warrior' and 'hero' are synonyms, and the main theme of a warrior culture is constructed on two notes—prowess and honour. The one is the hero's essential attribute, the other his essential aim. Every value, every judgement, every action, all skills and talents have the function of either defining honour or realizing it. Life itself may not stand in the way. The Homeric heroes loved life fiercely, as they did and felt everything with passion, and no less martyr-like characters could be imagined; but even life must surrender to honour. The two central figures of the *Iliad*, Achilles and Hector, were both fated to live short lives, and both knew it. They were heroes not because at the call of duty they marched proudly to their deaths, singing hymns to God and country—on the contrary, they railed openly against their doom, and Achilles, at least, did not complain less after he reached Hades—but because at the call of honour they obeyed the code of the hero without flinching and without questioning.

The heroic code was complete and unambiguous, so much so that neither the poet nor his characters ever had occasion to debate it. There were differences of opinion—whether to retreat in battle or not, whether to assassinate Telemachus or not, whether Osysseus was alive or dead — but these were either disagreements over matters of fact or tactical alternatives. In neither case was extended discussion called for. Or there were critical situations in which the knowledge available to mortals was insufficient, such as the plague that Apollo brought upon the Achaeans when they dishonoured his priest. Then it was necessary to seek answer from the gods, and that fell to the soothsayer Calchas (among the Trojans there was Hector's brother Helenus, skilled in interpreting the flight of birds). Again there was no occasion for genuine discussion: the soothsayer gave the answer, and the heroes either obeyed or they did not, as their hearts bade them. Finally, there were moments when even the greatest of the heroes knew fear, but then it was enough to cry 'Coward, woman!' to bring him back to his senses.

The significant fact is that never in either the *Iliad* or the *Odyssey* is there a rational discussion, a sustained, disciplined consideration of circumstances and their implications, of possible courses of action, their advantages and disadvantages. There are lengthy arguments, as between Achilles and Agamemnon, or between Telemachus and the suitors, but they are quarrels, not discussions, in which each side seeks to overpower the other by threats, and to win over the assembled multitude by emotional appeal, by harangue, and by warning. Skill with words had its uses in the struggle for public opinion — Phoenix reminded Achilles that it was he who had taught the latter 'to be both a speaker of words and a doer of deeds' (IX 443).

The figure of Nestor is perhaps the most revealing in this regard. Eventually Nestor became the prototype of the wisdom of old age, the voice of experience, but not once in his interminable talking did Homer's Nestor draw upon his experience as the ground for choice between alternative procedures. In fact, throughout the *Iliad* he made but one suggestion that could in any proper sense be called a significant and reasoned one, his proposal that the Achaeans build a great defensive wall before their camp on the beach. With that single exception, Nestor's talk was invariably emotional and psychological, aimed at bolstering morale or at soothing overheated tempers, not at selecting the course of action. For the former, his years of experience were very important, but in the unique sense of giving him the greatest store of incidents upon which to draw for models of heroic behaviour, for reminders by example of the way to honour and glory. Odysseus, on the other hand, was the man of many devices, and his superior skill in that respect took the form of deception and mendacity. 'Deceit and artful tales', Athena told him, not in criticism, 'are dear to you from the bottom of your heart' (13.295) Odysseus lied all the time, on the assumption that it could do no harm and might turn out useful in the end; and he lied cleverly. This may have been purposeful deception in a general sense, but it was not controlled rational behaviour. It was surely not wisdom.

The modern reader may be misled by the numerous formulas which, in one or another variant, speak of a man of counsel. For us counsel is deliberation; wise counsel, deliberation based on knowledge, experience, rational analysis, judgement. But counsel for Homer pointed less to the reasons than to the decision itself, and hence to the power of authority. Only in that sense could Nestor have called Agamemnon and Achilles 'first of the Danaans both in counsel and in battle' (1 258). Neither was preeminent in the giving of advice — Achilles particularly not — but by status and power they outranked the others in the right of decision. There was much talk about a king's seeking counsel; and there was scarcely any offered that was more than encouragement or admonition. After all, the basic values of the society were given, predetermined, and so were a man's place in the society and the privileges and duties that followed from his status. They were not subject to analysis or debate, and other issues left only the narrowest margin for the exercise of what we should call judgement (as distinct from work skills, including knowledge of the tactics of armed combat).

There were situations in which one could legitimately disagree whether or not the counsel of prudence was also the voice of cowardice. Then it was not a question of mere tactics, nor the illegitimate one of challenging or defending the code of honour, but a matter of properly classifying and evaluating a specific choice of procedures. In the *Iliad* prudence was personified in the Trojan Polydamas (not in Nestor), and his interchanges with Hector underscored the true quality of the hero. Polydamas urged caution: Do not attack the Achaeans lest Achilles be roused and return to the fight and destroy us all. This was the prudent road to success, and Hector was utterly impatient with it, for it was not the road of honour. Polydamas was right, of course, and thanks to Hector's imprudent heroism the poem soon reached the final stage of preparation before the decisive single combat between Hector and Achilles.

Prudence made one last attempt, this time in the persons of Priam and Hecuba, who begged their son not to fight Achilles, for the outcome was certain: Hector would be slain and Troy destroyed. Hector knew they were right in their prediction, as Polydamas had been earlier, and he said as much, but in a long soliloquy he rejected their plea and re-asserted the paramount claim of honour. 'I am ashamed before the Trojan men and the women of trailing robes, lest one worse than I should say: "Hector by trusting in his own might has destroyed the people."' What if I were to offer surrender and promise to return Helen and all her possessions and to pay in amends half the wealth of Troy? Achilles 'would kill me, unarmed, as if but a woman' (XXII 105-25).

Rather than that, Hector chose honourable death by combat, and the end of his city and his people. Once when Polydamas pointed to an ill omen as ground for caution, Hector brushed him off with 'One omen is best, to fight back for one's fatherland' (XII 243). But his whole course of behaviour gave the lie to that retort.* The fact is that such a notion of social obligation is fundamentally non-heroic. It reflects the new element, the community, at the one point at which it was permitted to override everything else, the point of defence against an invader. In the following generations, when the community began to move from the wings to the centre of the Greek stage, the hero quickly died out, for the honour of the hero was purely individual, something

---

* The constituent elements of 'fatherland' soon turn out to be, again in Hector's words (XV 496-9), wife, children, *oikos*, and landed estate.

he lived and fought for only for its sake and his own sake. (Family attachment was permissible, but that was because one's kin were indistinguishable from oneself). The honour of a community was a totally different quality, requiring another order of skills and virtues: in fact, the community could grow only by taming the hero and blunting the free exercise of his prowess, and a domesticated hero was a contradiction in terms.

Achilles, as a leader of the *invading* army, was not enmeshed in the extraneous strands of obligation. Writing long after Homer, Aeschylus could invent a scene (in a play now lost) in which the Myrmidons rebelled against Achilles for his refusal to fight. The Athenian playwright thus injected the notion of duty into the tale, but not once did Homer or Agamemnon or Odysseus charge Achilles with anything so anachronistic as public responsibility. Achilles was honour-bound to bring his incomparable prowess into the battle. But when Agamemnon took the girl Briseis from him his honour was openly shamed, and once 'honour is destroyed the moral existence of the loser collapses'.* The dilemma became at once unbearable: honour pulled in two opposing directions, and though one way pointed to victory in a great war and the other to a trifle, one captive woman out of thousands, the tremendous conflict lay precisely in the fact that honour was not measured like goods in a market, that the insult was worth as much as the war. Briseis was a trifle, but Briseis seized from Achilles was worth 'seven tripods that have never been on the fire and ten talents of gold and twenty glittering cauldrons' and twelve prize-winning race-horses and twenty Trojan captives and seven cities and a few other odds and ends (IX 121-56).

It was when Achilles refused this proper, and under all normal circumstances satisfactory, gift of amends that the real tragedy of the *Iliad* began. 'Sing, goddess, of the wrath of Peleus's son Achilles.' The hero's mistake was not made at the beginning; it came at the refusal of the penal gift, for that marked him as a man of unacceptable excesses, shameless in breaching the heroic code. 'Why,' said Ajax in indignation, 'a man even accepts

* Bruno Snell, *The Discovery of the Mind*, translated by T. G. Rosenmeyer (Oxford: Basil Blackwell, 1953), p. 160.

amends from the murderer of his brother or for his dead son, and the killer remains in his own country, having paid much. . . . But for you, the gods have put an implacable and evil emotion in your breast on account of a single girl' (IX 632-8). Homer could not close the tale with the death of Hector at the hands of Achilles, for that would have left us with Achilles the too angry man, not with Achilles the redeemed hero. Achilles had still to expunge his wrath. This he did by abandoning his idea of throwing Hector's body to the dogs—a new excess, stemming from his grief over the death of Patroclus—and by returning the body to Priam for the proper rites. Now the slate was clean. Achilles had vindicated his honour on all sides, and had done so both honourably and with the fullest display of his prowess.

It is in the nature of honour that it must be exclusive, or at least hierarchic. When everyone attains equal honour, then there is no honour for anyone. Of necessity, therefore, the world of Odysseus was fiercely competitive, as each hero strove to outdo the others. And because the heroes were warriors, competition was fiercest where the highest honour was to be won, in individual combat on the field of battle. There a hero's ultimate worth, the meaning of his life, received its final test in three parts: whom he fought, how he fought, and how he fared. Hence, as Thorstein Veblen phrased it, under 'this common-sense barbarian appreciation of worth or honour, the taking of life . . . is honourable in the highest degree. And this high office of slaughter, as an expression of the slayer's prepotence, casts a glamour of worth over every act of slaughter and over all the tools and accessories of the act.'* The *Iliad* in particular is saturated in blood, a fact which cannot be hidden or argued away, twist the evidence as one may in a vain attempt to fit archaic Greek values to a more gentle code of ethics. The poet and his audience lingered lovingly over every act of slaughter: 'Hippolochus darted away, and him too he [Agamemnon] smote to the ground; slicing off his hands with the sword and cutting off his neck, he sent him rolling like a round log through the battle-throng' (XI 145-7).

* *The Theory of the Leisure Class* (New York: Modern Library, 1934; London: Allen & Unwin, 1924), p. 18.

To Nietzsche the constant repetition of such scenes and their popularity throughout the Greek world for centuries to come demonstrated that 'the Greeks, the most humane men of ancient times, have a trait of cruelty, a tigerish lust to annihilate'.* But what must be stressed about Homeric cruelty is its heroic quality, not its specifically Greek character. In the final analysis, how can prepotence be determined except by repeated demonstrations of success? And the one indisputable measure of success is a trophy. While a battle is raging only the poet can observe Agamemnon's feat of converting Hippolochus into a rolling log. The other heroes are too busy pursuing glory for themselves. But a trophy is lasting evidence, to be displayed at all appropriate occasions. Among more primitive peoples the victim's head served that honorific purpose; in Homer's Greece armour replaced heads. That is why time after time, even at great personal peril, the heroes paused from their fighting in order to strip a slain opponent of his armour. In terms of the battle itself such a procedure was worse than absurd, it might jeoparize the whole expedition. It is a mistake in our judgement, however, to see the end of the battle as the goal, for victory without honour was unacceptable; there could be no honour without public proclamation, and there could be no publicity without the evidence of a trophy.

In different ways this pattern of honour-contest-trophy reappeared in every activity. Achilles could find no more fitting way to mourn his dead comrade than to set up a competitive situation in which the Achaean nobles might display their athletic prowess. The moment Diomedes brought his chariot to the finishing line in first place he leaped to the ground and 'he lost no time; . . . eagerly he took the prize and gave his high-spirited companions the woman to lead away and the tripod with handles to carry; and he unyoked the horses' (XXIII 510-13). This unselfconscious delight in the prizes, demonstrated before the excited assemblage, had little to do with their intrinsic worth; Diomedes, like Achilles,

---

* *Homer's Contest*, in *The Portable Nietzsche*, translated and edited by Walter Kaufmann (New York: Viking, 1954; London: Chatto & Windus, 1971), p. 32.

had slave women and tripods enough in his hut. His impetuosity — he did not even stop to attend to his horses — was an emotional response, open and unabashed, honour triumphant. We might call it a boyish gesture; for Diomedes it was pride in his manliness.

The contest was to play a tremendous part in Greek public life in later centuries. Nothing defines the quality of Greek culture more neatly than the way in which the idea of competition was extended from physical prowess to the realm of the intellect, to feats of poetry and dramatic composition. For that step the world of Odysseus was of course unprepared. It was also unprepared to socialize the contest, so to speak. Diomedes sought victory in the chariot race, as on the battlefield, for himself alone, for the honour of his name and in a measure for the glory of his kin and companions. Later, when the community principle gained mastery, the *polis* shared in the glory, and in turn it arranged for victory songs and even public statues to commemorate the honour it, the city, had gained through one of its athletic sons. And with the dilution of the almost pure egoism of heroic honour with civic pride went still another change for which the Homeric world was unprepared: the olive wreath and the laurel took the place of gold and copper and captive women as the victor's prize.*

Prestige symbols have a complex history. Among many primitive peoples they may be objects of little or no intrinsic worth, cowrie shells or wampum or cheap blankets. The world of Odysseus was not a primitive world, and in their higher sphere the Greeks of that time insisted on treasure. Their goal was honour, and the signs of honour are always conventional; but they would have nothing to do with conventional signs like cowrie. A beautiful young captive was a more honorific trophy than an old woman, and that was all there was to it. Even when the use of treasure was in display, in its prestige function, only its intrinsic worth gave it proper value.

Gift-giving too was part of the network of competitive, hono-

---

* Not many centuries were to pass, it must be added, before the post-Homeric Greeks were compelled to supplement the victors' wreaths with cash bonuses (awarded by the native cities, not by the management of the Olympic or Pythian Games).

rific activity. And in both directions: it was as honourable to give as to receive. One measure of a man's true worth was how much he could give away in treasure. Heroes boasted of the gifts they had received and of those they had given as signs of their prowess. That is why gift-objects had genealogies. When Telemachus refused Menelaus's offer of horses, the Spartan king countered with the following proposal: 'Of the gifts, such as are treasures lying in my house. I will give you the one which is finest and most valuable. I will give you a skilfully wrought bowl; it is all of silver, finished with gold on the rim, the work of Hephaestus. The hero Phaedimus, king of the Sidonians, gave it to me.'* A trophy with such a history obviously shed greater glory on both donor and recipient than just any silver bowl, as the armour of Hector was a far greater prize to his conqueror than the arms of one of the lesser Trojans. Status was the chief determinant of values, and status was transmitted from the person to his possessions, adding still more worth to their intrinsic value as gold or silver or fine woven cloth.

It was this honorific quality that distinguished the wealth of the heroes, and their almost overpowering accumulative instinct, from the materialistic drives of other classes and other ages. Wealth meant power and direct material satisfaction to Odysseus and his fellow-nobles, to be sure, and that equation was never absent from their calculations. When Odysseus awakened on Ithaca, where the Phaeacians had landed him while he slept, he failed to recognize the island because Athena had covered it with a mist. His first reaction was one of anger that Alcinous and his men had broken faith and conducted him to some strange place. And almost in the same breath he began worry about the gifts they had given him, lest they be stolen. Athena then appeared, quickly straightened him out, and personally helped him hide the treasure in a cave. Later, in his first meeting with Penelope, Odysseus in disguise deliberately misled her with an elaborate tale which ended with the story that he had but recently met the long-lost hero in Thesprotia, from which country 'he is bringing much good treasure as he begs up and down the land'.

* 1.374-5, repeated 2.239-40.

He would have returned sooner, 'but it seemed to his heart more advantageous to collect much goods as he went over the earth' (19.272-84).

The tale was false, but as the poet said, it was 'in the likeness of truth' (19.203). Odysseus actually used the verb 'to beg' (*aitizo*), the very word employed by Eumaeus when he advised his disguised master to go into town and beg for food. But what Odysseus meant and what Eumaeus meant were altogether different. A king 'begged' for gifts of treasure as part of the normal course of his travels and his relations abroad, with kin and guest-friends, old and new, as a way of adding new links to the endless chain of gift and counter-gift. When King Alcinous asked him to remain overnight so that the proper parting gifts could be assembled, Odysseus replied: I would wait a year if necessary, 'for more advantageous would it be to come to my dear fatherland with a fuller hand, and so should I be more reverenced and loved among men, whosoever should see me after I returned to Ithaca' (11.358-61). This he said in the same court in which he had reacted so violently to the suggestion that he might be a trader seeking 'coveted gains'.

There were delicate distinctions here, between honourable acquisition and a trader's gain. The heroes had a streak of the peasant in them, and with it went a peasant's love of possessions, a calculating, almost niggardly hoarding and measuring and counting. Wealth was an unequivocal good; the more wealth, the greater the good, a subject for boasting, not for concealment. But the heroes were more than peasants, and they could give as proudly as they took, and they could set honour above all material goods. The same Achilles who reminded Agamemnon that 'it was not on account of the Trojan warriors that I came here to fight, for they have committed no offence against me; they have not robbed me of my cattle or my horses' (I 152-4), could reject with contempt Agamemnon's compensatory gifts, fabulous as they were: 'For cattle and fine sheep can be rustled, and tripods and chestnut horses can be acquired' (IX 406-7). The circulation of treasure was as essential a part of heroic life as its acquisition; and it was this movement, the fact of its existence and the orbits it followed, that set that life apart from any other life of accumulation.

What tends to confuse us is the fact that the heroic world was unable to visualize any achievement or relationship except in concrete terms. The gods were anthropomorphized, the emotions and feelings were located in specific organs of the body, even the soul was materalized. Every quality or state had to be translated into some specific symbol, honour into a trophy, friendship into treasure, marriage into gifts of cattle. In the furious quarrel with Agamemnon, Achilles reached such a point of wrath that he drew his sword. Athena promptly appeared beside him, unseen to anyone else, and checked him with a command curiously put in the language of a plea, and ending with these words: 'For thus do I declare, and it shall come to pass: hereafter shall splendid gifts come to you in threefold measure, because of this [Agamemnon's] insolence; but restrain yourself and hearken to us' (1 212-4). This was the only intelligible language of pleading, and by gifts the goddess meant material goods, not blessings of the spirit.

Because the concrete expressions of honour and friendship were always articles of intrinsic value, not cowrie shells, the prestige element was concealed under an overlay of treasure. In fact, both counted greatly, the wealth on the one hand, and the wealth as symbol on the other. That is why the giving and receiving were ceremonial acts, an added touch that would have been needless were possession sufficient unto itself. King Alcinous personally stowed the Phaeacian gifts aboard Odysseus's ship, as the head of a modern state personally signs a treaty before assembled dignitaries. In a significant sense the gifts of guest-friendship were the archaic forerunners of articles of agreement. What other firm proof could there have been, in that unlettered world, that a relationship had been established, creating obligations and responsibilities?

At no point was the bond between ceremonialism and the satisfaction of material wants more tightly knit than in the endless feasting. 'For I say that there is nothing more gracious than when one has good cheer among the whole population, and the sharers in the feast in all the homes, seated in order, listen to the minstrel, and the tables alongside them are laden with bread and meat, and the cupbearer draws wine from the mixing-bowl and serves it around and pours it into the goblets' (9.5-10). Odysseus was weary. After ten years of war and another ten years of the most incredible and taxing adventures he had come to the Phaeacian Utopia, and his mind was reaching out to his own home, to the approaching end of his wanderings. He began to relax, and he made this pretty little speech.

But there was more than good cheer and *Gemütlichkeit* to Homeric feasting. 'Idomeneus,' said Agamemnon, 'I honour you above all the Danaans of the fleet horses, whether in war or in some other work or in the feast, when the Argive nobles mix the sparkling wine of the elders in the bowl' (IV 257-70). This formulation of the hierarchy of aristocratic activities, setting the banquet alongside the battle and 'other work', was precise, for it was feasting that occupied the heroes when they were not immediately engaged in the pursuits of combat, and it was heroic feasting, not only in its magnitude but also in its ethics. What was blameworthy about the suitors, for example, was not the total idleness and luxury of their daily banqueting in the halls of Odysseus. That was proper aristocratic behaviour, but it was most improper to carry on the feasting at one man's expense, all the more so when it was done in his absence. 'Sharers in the feast' was the phrase (one word in the Greek) Odysseus used in Phaeacia, and by it he meant those who shared the cost as well as the pleasures. 'Leave my palace,' Telemachus demanded of the suitors in all earnestness, with no trace of mockery, 'and hold your feasts elsewhere, eating your own substance, going from house to house in turn.'*

Just as there could be no ceremonial occasion without gifts of treasure, so there could be none without a feast. The *Iliad* closes with the Trojan mourning for Hector. For nine days they mourned, and on the tenth they cremated his body, placed the bones in a golden urn, and buried them in the presence of the assembled Trojan army. 'And having heaped the burial mound, they went back; then they gathered and feasted well in a glorious

* 1.374-5, repeated 2.139-40.

feast in the house of Priam, the king nourished by Zeus. Thus they performed the funeral rites for Hector, tamer of horses' (xxiv 801-4). Or, to take a different example, there is Nestor's advice to Agamemnon: 'Give a feast for the elders, that is proper for you and not unseemly' (ix 70). On such occasions, of course, there was no sharing of cost; Priam gave the feast that closed the funeral rites, and Agamemnon feasted his council of elders before they deliberated.

The meaning of this ceremonial eating together becomes clearest in still another context. Without exception, whenever a visitor arrived, whether kin or guest-friend, emissary or stranger, the first order of business was the sharing of a meal. This was a rule on all levels, when Odysseus, Ajax, and Phoenix came to Achilles with Agamemnon's proposal of a gift of amends, or when the then unidentified beggar appeared at the hut of Eumaeus the slave and swineherd. Only after the meal was it proper for the host to inquire who his guest was and what his mission. 'But come along,' said Eumaeus, 'let us go into the hut, old man, so that after you have satisfied yourself with bread and wine to your heart's content, you may tell whence you are and how many troubles you have suffered' (14.45-7).

This was a ritual that could not be refused, akin to the taboo-purging rituals of the primitive world. Hence the meal was shared not merely by host and guest and their retainers, but also by the gods. 'Then the swineherd stood up and carved ... and he divided and distributed the whole into seven portions. The first he set aside for the nymphs and for Hermes son of Maia, having prayed, and the others he distributed to each ... and he made burnt offering to the everlasting gods' (14.432-6). The descriptions of the sacrifices vary, and so do the names of the participating gods, but the essential notion was always the same. Through the sharing of food—in substantial quantities, it should be noted, not just symbolically—a bond was instituted, or renewed, in ceremonial fashion, tying men and gods, the living and the dead, into an ordered universe of existence. It was as if the constant repetition of the feast were somehow necessary for the preservation of the group, whether on the *oikos* level or on the larger scale of the class, and also for the establishment of peaceful relations across lines, with strangers and guest-friends.

Conversely, exclusion from the feast was a mark of the social outcast. Upon learning of the death of Hector, Andromache in her great grief lamented the fate in store for the boy Astyanax: 'And in his need the child turns to his father's companions, pulling one by the cloak, another by the tunic; and of those who take pity one gives him a sip, and he moistens his lips, but his palate he does not moisten. And some unorphaned child drives him from the feast with blows of the hand, reviling him with abuse: "Away, you! Your father does not share the feast with us"' (XXII 492-8).

Andromache could not protect her child, not even in her imagination, for women had no place at the feast. Not only was this a man's world, it was one in which the inferior status of women was neither concealed nor idealized, which knew neither chivalry nor romantic attachments. 'Do they then alone of mortal men love their wives, these sons of Atreus?' Achilles is quoted as asking, according to the usual translations.* The Greek, however, does not say 'wives', it says 'bed-mates'; Achilles was speaking of a woman he had 'won with the spear'. Earlier Agamemnon had said of Chryseis, the priest's captive daughter, 'Yes, I prefer her to Clytaemnestra, my wedded bed-mate' (I 113-4). In fact, from Homer to the end of Greek literature there were no ordinary words with the specific meanings 'husband' and 'wife'. A man was a man, a father, a warrior, a nobleman, a chieftain, a king, a hero; linguistically he was almost never a husband.

And then there is the word 'to love'. That is how we render *philein*, but the question remains open as to what emotional quality, what overtones, the Greek verb really possessed. It was used in every context in which there were positive ties between people. When he visited Aeolus, keeper of the winds, Odysseus reported, 'he treated me hospitably for a full month' (10.14), and *philein* was the word by which hospitable treatment was expressed. But where in the many references to Odysseus's sad longing for his home and his wife is there a passage in which sentiments and passions that the modern world calls 'love' shine through? More

* IX 340-1, in the translation by A. T. Murray in the *Loeb Classical Library*.

often than not Penelope was omitted from the image of home, for the standard formula was the one used by Nausicaa: 'Then there is hope that you will see your friends, and come to your home good to dwell in, and to your native land.'*

Odysseus was fond of Penelope, beyond a doubt, and he found her sexually desirable. She was part of what he meant by 'home', the mother of his dear son and the mistress of his *oikos*. Monogamous marriage was the rule.† There are no confirmed bachelors in the poems and no spinsters, and the sole reference to divorce is the somewhat dubious one in which Hephaestus threatened to return his adulterous wife, Aphrodite, to her father (a threat that was not carried out) (8.317-20). The meaning of monogamy must not be misconstrued, however. It neither imposed monogamous sexuality on the male nor did it place the small family at the centre of a man's emotional life. The language had no word for the small family, in the sense in which one might say, 'I want to go back to live with my family.'

Neither in the relationship between Odysseus and Penelope nor in any other relationship between man and mate in the Homeric poems was there the depth and intensity, the quality of feeling — on the part of the male — that marked the attachment between father and son on the one hand, and between male and male companion on the other. The poems are rich in such images as this: 'as a father greets his dear son who has come from a distant land in the tenth year' (16.17-18); but there are no similes drawn from a husband's joy in his wife. In the narrative itself one need only recall the key role of the love of Achilles for Patroclus, and the massive grief of Achilles at the death of his comrade.

There is an ancient dispute, still unresolved, whether overt eroticism was part of the relationship between Achilles and Patroclus. The text of the poems offers no directly affirmative evidence at any point; even the two references to the elevation of

---

* 6.314-5; repeated by Athena 7.76-7, and used earlier by Zeus, 5.41-2, and by Hermes, 5.114-5.

† The sole 'exception', Priam with his several wives, fifty sons, twelve daughters and uncounted grandchildren, is as mysterious to us as it may have been to the poet. No other man is polygamous, *not even in Troy*, nor is any god.

Ganymede to Olympus speak only of his becoming cupbearer to Zeus. Pederasty was a widely accepted practice in the Greek world at a very early date, and it remained an integral part of Greek culture for many centuries, as the literature from Theognis to Plato eloquently testifies. What was involved, furthermore, was not homosexuality in the sense of the direction of erotic impulses and activity exclusively to members of one's own sex, but a full bisexuality. Neither Greek practice nor Greek ethics, therefore, would have seen anything inconsistent or unlikely in the coexistence of an erotic relationship between heroes and their vaunted prowess with the opposite sex. If historical proof is needed it is enough to point to the warrior élite of Thebes. And so, to explain the striking intensity of Achilles' passion and to fit the world of Odysseus into the mainstream of Hellenic culture, it has been argued that on this matter we are faced with an instance of 'expurgation' in the poems, that 'Homer has swept this whole business, root and branch, out of his conception of life'.*

Be that as it may, there is no mistaking the fact that Homer fully reveals what remained true for the whole of antiquity, that women were held to be naturally inferior and therefore limited in their function to the production of offspring and the performance of household duties, and that the meaningful social relationships and the strong personal attachments were sought and found among men. The classic exposition may be read in the eighth book of Aristotle's *Nicomachean Ethics*, on *philia*, which we render with the pale word 'friendship'. When there is *philia* of a lower kind, says Aristotle, between unequal partners, as between a man and a woman, 'each of the two differs in virtue and function, in the ground for friendship, and therefore also in affection and friendship. Accordingly, the affection should be proportionate to the respective worths of each: 'the better [of the two], for example, should receive more affection than he gives'. And that is precisely what we find in Homer. While Odysseus was absent the loss to Penelope, emotionally, psychologically,

* Gilbert Murray, *The Rise of the Greek Epic* (3rd edn., Oxford: Clarendon Press, 1924), p. 125. Other examples of possible 'expurgation' will be noticed below.

affectively, was incomparably greater than the loss to her husband. The grief of Achilles was nearly matched by the sorrow of Hecuba and Andromache at the death of Hector, son to one and husband to the other.

Some caution must be exercised here. What we have is a skilfully shaped portrayal of the second sex, in which a bard who shared the conviction of the natural inferiority of women defined their feelings to their lords and superiors. The image which emerges is a complicated one, and in some respects an enigmatic one. The two characters in the poems who are not fully resolved are both women, Arete, queen of the Phaeacians, with her strange unwomanly claims to power and authority, and Helen, who is a very peculiar figure. Helen, daughter of Zeus and Leda, was Aphrodite's favourite, and thanks to the gifts of the goddess she succeeded in embroiling Greeks and Trojans in a gigantic struggle that cost both sides dearly. Helen was no innocent victim in all this, no unwilling captive of Paris-Alexander, but an adulteress in the most complete sense. For Paris there was no atonement. 'Lord Zeus,' prayed Menelaus, 'grant that I be avenged on him who first did me wrong, illustrious Alexander, and subdue him at my hands, so that any man born hereafter may shrink from wronging a host who has shown him friendship' (III 351-4). But Helen received no punishment, and scarcely any reproach. She ended her days back in Sparta, administering magical drugs obtained in Egypt, interpreting omens, and participating in the life of the palace much like Arete and not like a proper Greek woman.

Not even Penelope was altogether free of suspicion and the element of enigma. When Athena bade Telemachus return immediately from his visit to Menelaus, lest Penelope, who was weakening under pressure from her father and brothers, not only accept one of the suitors but strip the palace of treasure to boot, the goddess concluded with a sweeping generalization: 'For you know what is the emotion in the breast of a woman, that she wishes to increase the household of him who weds her, and of her former children and of her dear husband she neither remembers once he is dead nor inquires' (15.20-3).

This was a strange way indeed to talk about Penelope, and

it came from a very interesting source. On Olympus the gods were altogether superior to the goddesses, considered collectively —superior not only in their power but also in their appeal, in the feelings they inspired among men. The chief exception to the rule was Athena, and the significant quality of Athena as a goddess was her manliness. She was the virgin goddess in a world that knew no original sin, no sinfulness of sex, no Vestal Virgins. She was not even born of woman, having sprung from the head of Zeus—an insult to the whole race of women for which Hera never forgave her husband, Hera who was the complete female and whom the Greeks feared a little and did not like at all, from the days of Odysseus to the twilight of the gods.

Neither Athena nor the poet went further in explaining Penelope's behaviour. The responsibility for Helen, however, was explicitly Aphrodite's. Early in the *Iliad*, Paris engaged Menelaus in single combat and was within an inch of losing his life when 'Aphrodite snatched him up most easily, being a god, and covered him with a heavy mist and set him down in his fragrant, incense-smelling chamber. And she herself went to summon Helen' from the battlements. '"Come here. Alexander summons you to go home. He is there in his chamber and inlaid bed."' Helen demurred. 'Then angrily divine Aphrodite addressed her: "Do not provoke me, wretch, lest in my wrath I abandon you, and in this wise hate you as now I love you beyond measure"' (III 380-415). And Helen was afraid, and she took herself to the fragrant chamber and the inlaid bed.

The reason for Helen's reluctance had been given some verses before. In the guise of Laodice, Priam's fairest daughter, the divine messenger Iris had talked with her and had 'placed in her heart sweet yearning for her former husband and her city and parents' (III 139-40). This impasse in which Helen was placed was nothing unusual, for in the Homeric psychology every human action and every idea could be the direct consequence of divine intervention. In ordinary affairs one could never be sure (and a man could anyway fail to grasp or to follow the divine guide-line). Thus, in reply to Penelope's request for an explanation of Telemachus's risky journey to Pylos and Sparta in search of news of his father, the herald Medon said (4.712-3): 'I do not know whether some god urged him on, or whether his own heart (*thymos*) stirred him to go to Pylos.'

However, when the action was witless or otherwise astonishing, there was no doubt that the gods had intervened. When Eurycleia informed Penelope that Odysseus had returned and destroyed the suitors, the queen replied in utter disbelief: 'Good mother, the gods have made you mad, they who are able to make witless even those with the best wit, and they bring the weakminded to prudence. They have distracted you, who were formerly right-minded' (23.11-14). The examples can be multiplied from every page and every conceivable situation.

Nowhere is the historian faced with a more subtle problem. Was all this literal belief or poetic metaphor? When the heroes are called *dios* (divine), *isotheos* (god-equal), *diotrephes* (nourished by Zeus), precisely what significance shall we attach to the epithets?* What did they mean to the poet and his audience? When Menelaus began to drag Paris in the dust and Aphrodite tore off the latter's helmet-strap just before it strangled him, was that a fancy poetic figure for chance, for a lucky accident that broke the strap in time, or did Homer believe literally what he sang? What *we* believe in these matters is irrelevant and misleading. Modern critics who call Homer's gods 'symbolic predicates', the activity on Olympus the poet's 'scenario', not only inject modern theology and modern science into the world of Odysseus, they destroy the poems. The narrative itself collapses without the interventions of the gods, and so do the psychology and the behaviour of the heroes.

A fair test is provided by the genealogies, which gave most aristocratic families, and even whole tribes, divine ancestry. Poseidon was angered beyond measure by the Phaeacians because they not only rescued Odysseus but returned him to Ithaca laden with treasure, and his anger was compounded by the fact that the Phaeacians 'come from my own stock' (13.130). In Odysseus's account of his journey to Hades there is one lengthy

* Following an accepted convention, I have translated *dios* as 'illustrious' throughout.

section which parades various women proud to have borne mortal sons to Zeus or Poseidon. The converse was exceedingly rare—Calypso even protested: 'You are merciless, you gods, and jealous beyond compare, who begrudge goddesses that they have intercourse with men openly, if one makes one her dear bedfellow' (5.118-20). From one such union came Achilles, son of Peleus and of Thetis the sea-nymph; from another, Aeneas, son of Anchises and Aphrodite.

It is inconceivable that this passion for divine genealogy was mere poetic fancy. Here was sanction for aristocratic privilege, for rule by might, and an ideology that no one believes is an absurdity. Xenophanes, in the sixth century, was not tilting at windmills when he raised his voice in the sharpest possible protest against the Homeric view of the gods. If 'theft, adultery and deceit' were commonly accepted as divine practices, then surely divine ancestry of mortals and divine intervention in battle were scarcely less credible. The irrelevance of so many of the interventions, which contribute nothing to the development of the narrative, is a further argument. Presumably there is much here that was part of the inherited bardic formulas, repeated and perpetuated after much of primitive belief had degenerated into mere clichés of speech and story-telling. The essential difficulty is to find the proper line between a thought-world that was gone and a rationality that was yet to come.

One element which deserves particular notice is the complete anthropomorphism. God was created in man's image with a skill and a genius that must be ranked with man's greatest intellectual feats. The whole of heroic society was reproduced on Olympus in its complexities and its shadings. The world of the gods was a social world in every respect, with a past and a present, with a history, so to speak. There was no Genesis, no creation out of nothing. The gods came to power on Olympus as men came to power in Ithaca or Sparta or Troy, through struggle or family inheritance. Here is the account in Poseidon's words (xv 187-93) of what followed the forcible overthrow of the Titans: 'For we are three brothers, sons of Cronus, whom Rhea bore, Zeus and I, and Hades is the third, who rules the underworld. And in three lots we divided everything, and each drew his share of honour [i.e. his domain]: I drew the white sea to inhabit forever, when we cast lots, and Hades drew the murky darkness, and Zeus drew the wide heaven, in air and clouds; but the earth and high Olympus are common to all' (xv 187-93).

These sentences were part of a very angry speech. Poseidon had entered the battle on the Greek side, and the Trojans were in rout. Zeus sent Iris to him with an order that he withdraw from the fight. 'Highly indignant, the renowned earth-shaker answered her: "Oh no, for strong as he is, he has spoken insolently if he will master me by force, against my will, I who am his equal in honour"' (xv 184-6). Poseidon gave in, of course, but in the colloquy the parallel between gods and heroes was perfectly drawn. Like any hero, Poseidon was concerned solely with honour and prowess. He bowed to the authority of Zeus, but only because the elder brother was prepotent. Earlier, when Hera first proposed that together they could outmanoeuvre Zeus and save the Achaeans from the slaughter that was planned for them, Poseidon would have none of it. 'Hera reckless in speech, what manner of talk have you spoken! I would not see us all at war with Zeus Cronion, for he is far greater' (viii 209-11).

With respect to power, the divine world was as differentiated as the human, and the range was very wide. Not only were there great differences in the quantity possessed by the individual gods, there were also significant distinctions in the spheres in which power could be applied. Aphrodite, for example, was invincible in matters of erotic desire. But when she tried to take part in the actual fighting, Diomedes attacked her, 'knowing that she was a feeble god' (v 331), and he wounded her in the hand. Aphrodite went weeping to Zeus, only to receive a gentle rebuke: 'Not to you, my child, are given the works of war, but do you pursue the loving works of wedlock and all these will be looked to by fleet Ares and Athena' (v 428-30).

Only Zeus occupied a position without earthly parallel. Although he was not perfect, neither omnipotent nor omniscient — that must be underscored — his power was overwhelming, beyond the dreams of even the greatest king. And Zeus maintained a distance between himself and the mortal world that was also unique. He alone of the Olympians never intervened directly in speech or act, but through a verbal message carried by Iris, Dream, Rumour, or one of the other gods, or through the still less direct form of an omen, such as thunder or the flight of an eagle. Even on Olympus there was distance: when Zeus entered his palace, 'all the gods rose at once from their seats in the presence of their father' (1 533-4). It would be a mistake, however, to imagine Zeus as some kind of Eastern super-potentate. For all his uniqueness, he had much of the Greek *basileus* in him (though Homer never gave him the title), a special sort of first among equals. The *Odyssey* opens with an appeal by Athena that he put an end to the travail of Odysseus. In reply Zeus first denied responsibility for what was happening. 'It is Poseidon the earth-mover who has stubbornly remained angry, because of the Cyclops whom he [Odysseus] blinded in the eye.' Then Zeus proposed a course of action: 'But come, let us all here consider his homecoming, that he might return. Poseidon will give up his anger, for he will be powerless against all the immortals, striving alone against the will of the gods' (1.68-79).

This mixture of might and counsel bespoke the archaic world. Even Poseidon admitted the power of Zeus to compel obedience, and yet the poet was reluctant to reduce the decision to force alone. He was not always able to achieve full consistency in the heavenly picture. The case of Zeus is outstanding, but there are others, such as the two conceptions of fate, one that it was the work of the gods and the other that it bound all, mortals and immortals alike (including Zeus because his knowledge fell short of omniscience); or the notion of Hades as neutral, as a place where the shades of men live on in utter dullness and emptiness, but where, nevertheless, a few like Tantalus are doomed to ever-lasting torment. The inconsistencies merely point up how tremendous was the effort to re-create the heroic world on another plane, and how very successful it was. The evidence can be drawn from every sphere, from wealth and labour, gift-giving and feasting, honour and shame.

A measure of failure was inevitable. That the gods were

immortal was one source of difficulty, but perhaps not the chief one. Because they could not die, the gods could not be true heroes. They might fail to attain a specific goal, but they could try again and again, and there was never any risk of death in the attempt. Still, it was possible to overlook that one flaw and to have the gods behave otherwise exactly as heroes would behave. It was possible, too, to take care of minor technicalities of immortality: blood was the physiological key to mortality, and therefore it had to be replaced by another substance, called ichor. What was not possible was to define power in purely human terms, even on the most heroic scale. Divine power was supernatural in the precise sense. It was superior to human power in its quality, in its magic. Diomedes could defeat Aphrodite in direct combat, but only so long as the feeble goddess failed to avail herself of the supernatural powers that even she commanded. She could have covered him with a heavy mist and snatched him up and away, for instance. Against such arts Achilles himself would have been outmatched. Only the gods, further, had the power to take a man's wits from him, or to teach bards and seers to know things that had been and things that were to be.

The humanization of the gods was a step of astonishing boldness. To picture supernatural beings not as vague, formless spirits, or as monstrous shapes, half bird, half animal, for instance, but as men and women, with human organs and human passions, demanded the greatest audacity and pride in one's own humanity. Then, having so created his gods, Homeric man called himself godlike. The words 'man' and 'godlike' must be stressed sharply. On the one hand, Homer never confused 'godlike' with 'divine'; he never crossed the line between the mortal and the immortal. Hesiod spoke of 'a godlike race of hero-men who are called demi-gods', but there were no demi-gods in the *Iliad* or *Odyssey*. Kings were honoured like gods, but never worshipped. Heroes were men, not cult objects. Though they had divine ancestors, blood ran in their veins none the less, not ichor. On the other hand, there were no local, regional or national dividing-lines of genuine consequence among men. Neither in matters of cult nor in any other fundamental aspect of human life did the poet distinguish or classify invidiously. Individuals and classes varied in worth and capacity, but not peoples, neither between Achaeans and others nor among the Achaeans themselves. This universality of Homer's humanity was as bold and remarkable as the humanity of his gods.

That we are faced here with a new creation, a revolution in religion, can scarcely be doubted. We do not know who accomplished it, but we can be sure that a sudden transformation had occurred, not just a slow, gradual shift in beliefs. Never in the history of the known religions, Eastern or Western, was a new religion introduced otherwise than at one stroke. New ideas may have been germinating for a long time, old ideas may have been undergoing constant and slow change, still other notions may have been imported from abroad. But the actual step of transformation, the creation of a new conceptual scheme, has always been sharp, swift, abrupt.

It is no underestimation of the magnitude of the revolution to add that it was far from complete. More precisely, it was not universal: the history of Greek religion in subsequent centuries shows great variation on this score, according to social class, education, individual temperament, circumstance. Xenophanes did not speak for the illiterate mountaineers of Arcadia or the semiliterate peasants of his native Colophon or his adopted Sicily. Age-old magical practices and cults, such as those associated with hot springs, continued to flourish. The pre-Olympian cosmological myths had a long life ahead. All the more remarkable, therefore, that the traces in the Homeric poems (in contrast to Hesiod) are so few as to warrant another reference to Homeric 'expurgations'. The old nature gods, for instance, were either debased or ignored. Helius, the sun, was so impotent that when Odysseus's starving men committed the terrible offence of killing some of his cattle he could do no better than rush to Zeus and ask the latter to take vengeance for him. Selene, the moon, was of no consequence whatsoever.

Most notable of all is the indifference to Demeter, goddess of fertility, for unlike Helius and Selene, Demeter remained a major figure in Greek religion for many centuries after Homer. Her rites celebrated the procession of the seasons, the mystery of the plants and the fruits in their annual cycle of coming to be and passing away. Demeter-worship was carried on outside the formal Olympian religion, for its founders had place neither for her nor for mystery rites altogether. Homer knew all about Demeter (she is mentioned six times in the *Iliad* and *Odyssey*); and that is just the point. He deliberately turned his back on her and everything she represented.

'Honour him like a god with gifts' is a recurrent phrase about kings; the converse is that the gods are to be honoured like kings with gifts. In practice that meant gifts of food, of feasting, through burnt offerings, and gifts of treasure, through dedications of arms and cauldrons and tripods arrayed in the temples. The temples and their priests, incidentally, were themselves part of the new religion. The forces of nature had been worshipped where they were; the gods conceived as men were housed, like men, in appropriate palaces. Mystery rites (literally 'orgies', a word which does not appear in either poem) and blood rites and human sacrifice and everything else that dehumanized the gods were ruthlessly discarded. Thus the important story of the sacrifice of Agamemnon's daughter Iphigenia was omitted, and the many gross atrocities in the prehistory of the gods were toned down radically. Achilles, it is true, sacrificed 'twelve brave sons of great-hearted Trojans' on the funeral pyre of Patroclus, but the poet promptly labelled that act of primitive horror for what it was: 'such evil deeds did he contrive in his heart' (XXIII 175-6).

In a famous passage in his autobiography, John Stuart Mill wrote of his father: 'I have a hundred times heard him say that all ages and nations have represented their gods as wicked, in a constantly increasing progression; that mankind have gone on adding trait after trait till they reached the most perfect conception of wickedness which the human mind can devise, and have called this God, and prostrated themselves before it.' For Homeric religion, at least, this is not a pertinent judgement, not because Homer's gods were incapable of wickedness, but because they were essentially devoid of any ethical quality whatsoever. The ethics of the world of Odysseus were man-made and man-sanctioned. Man turned to the gods for help in his manifold activities, for the gifts it was in their power to offer or to withhold. He could not turn to them for moral guidance; that was not in their power. The Olympian gods had not created the world, and they were therefore not responsible for it.

When Odysseus awoke on Ithaca, Athena appeared to him in the guise of a shepherd and was greeted by one of Odysseus's characteristic inventions, how he came from Crete, fought at Troy, slew the son of Idomeneus, fled to the Phoenicians, and so forth. Athena smiled, resumed her female shape, and offered the following comment: 'Crafty must he be and shifty who would outstrip you in all kinds of cunning, even though it be a god that encountered you. Headstrong man, full of wiles, of cunning insatiate, are you not to cease, even in your own land, from deceit and artful tales, so dear to you from the bottom of your heart? But come, let us speak no more of these things, being both practised in craft; for you are far the best of all mortals in counsel and speech, and I am celebrated among all the gods in craft and cunning' (13.291-9).

This is what the line of philosophers from Xenophanes to Plato protested, the indifference of the Homeric gods in moral matters. Just before the close of the *Iliad* (XXIV 527-33), Achilles stated the doctrine explicitly: 'For two jars stand on Zeus's threshold whence he gives of his evil gifts, and another of the good; and to whom Zeus who delights in thunder gives a mixed portion, to him befalls now evil, now good; but to whom he gives of the baneful, him he scorns, and evil misery chases him over the noble earth, a wanderer honoured neither by gods nor by mortals.'

Chance, not merit, determined how the gifts fell to a man. And since it was not in his power to influence the choice, man could neither sin nor atone. He could offend a god mightily, but only by dishonouring him, by shaming him — through a false oath, for example, or disobedience of the direct command of an oracle or failure to make a sacrificial gift — and then it was incumbent upon the offender to make amends precisely as he made amends to any man he might have dishonoured. But this was not penance;

it was the re-establishment of the proper status relationship. Without sin there could be no idea of conscience, no feelings of moral guilt. The evils of which Achilles spoke were mishaps, not the evils of the Decalogue.

And there was no reverential fear of the gods. 'Homer's princes bestride their world boldly; they fear the gods only as they fear their human overlords.'* No word for 'god-fearing' is ever used in the *Iliad*. Nor, it scarcely need be added, was there a word for 'love of god': *philotheos* makes its first known appearance in the language with Aristotle. For moral support the men of the *Iliad* relied not on the gods but on their fellow-men, on the institutions and the customs by which they lived; so complete was the intellectual revolution that had occurred. Having lifted the incubus of unintelligible and all-powerful natural forces, man retained a consciousness that there were powers in the universe which he could not control and could not really understand, but he introduced a great self-consciousness, a pride and a confidence in himself, in man and his ways in society.

But what of the men whose life gave no warrant for pride and self-confidence? For it is self-evident that the gods of the *Iliad* were the gods of heroes, or, plainly spoken, of the princes and the heads of the great households. What of the others, those for whom the iron age had come, when 'men never rest from labour and sorrow by day, and from perishing by night'?† They had reason enough to fear the gods, but they had no reason to be god-fearing if the gods were truly as the poet described them. For them there was little question of choice of gifts; there was always the certainty that the gifts would come from the wrong jar: 'Evil misery chases him over the noble earth, a wanderer honoured neither by gods nor by mortals.' The poet of the *Iliad* could turn away from Demeter in contempt, but to the iron race of men she gave promise of a harvest, as the god Dionysus, whom Homer also ignored, meant wine and joy and forgetfulness of sorrow. 'Apollo moved only in the best society, from the days

* E. R. Dodds, *The Greeks and the Irrational* (University of California Press, 1951), p. 29.
† Hesiod, *Works and Days*, 176-8.

when he was Hector's patron to the days when he canonized aristocratic athletes; but Dionysus was at all periods *demotikos*, a god of the people.'*

The Olympian religion could not stand still and yet survive. The intellectual revolution reflected in the *Iliad* required still another revolution, a moral one, in which Zeus was transformed from the king of a heroic society to the principle of cosmic justice. There are elements of this new conception in the *Odyssey*, for the suitor theme is in some fashion a tale of villainy and retribution. 'Father Zeus,' said old Laertes when Odysseus revealed himself and told him of the slaughter of the suitors, 'indeed you gods still exist on high Olympus, if truly the wooers have paid for their evil insolence' (24.351-2). The contrast with the *Iliad* is striking. There the destruction of Troy was, if anything, an act of divine injustice. Paris had insulted Menelaus, and both sides, Achaeans and Trojans alike, were prepared at one point to rest the decision on single combat between the two heroes. Menelaus was the victor, and the war should have ended then, with the return of Helen and the payment of amends, but Hera and Athena would not be content until Ilion was sacked and all its men killed. The interest of the two goddesses was strictly heroic, an insistence on full retribution for the shame they once had suffered at the hands of Paris when he judged Aphrodite more beautiful. This and nothing else brought about the fall of Troy.

Zeus bowed to Hera's demand, even though, in his own words, 'of all the cities under the sun and the starry heaven in which dwell earthly men, most honoured of my heart was holy Ilion, and Priam and the people of Priam of the good ashen spear'. Hera responded in kind: 'Indeed there are three cities most dear of all to me, Argos and Sparta and widewayed Mycenae. May these waste whenever they become hateful to your heart; for them I shall neither stand up nor hold a grudge' (IV 44-54). For the decision to be put into effect, it should be added, Athena was called upon to trap the Trojans, by the most malicious deception, into violating the oaths they and the Achaeans had taken when Menelaus and Paris met in single combat.

* Dodds, *The Greeks and the Irrational*, p. 76.

From such a view of divine motives to the punishment of the
suitors was a long step, and the poet of the *Odyssey* took it hesi-
tantly and incompletely. Its implications were extensive and complex, and he did not always see them by any means. When he
did, the effect was startling. No sooner had Eurycleia returned
to the great chamber of the palace and seen the carnage among
the suitors than 'she was about to cry out in exultation, beholding
so great a deed. But Odysseus restrained her. . . . "Rejoice in
your heart, old woman, and restrain yourself and do not cry
aloud. It is an unholy thing to glory over slain men. These men
the destiny of the gods had overpowered, and their [own] merciless deeds"' (22.408-13). Not only was this sentiment unheroic,
for heroes commonly exercised their prerogative to exult publicly
over their victims, but in a sense it remained un-Hellenic, as
Nietzsche's dictum suggests. It was as if, groping to understand
a new vision of man and his fate, the poet saw something so profound, and yet so far beyond the horizon of his world, that he
gave it expression in a few brief verses, only to draw back from
it at once.

Interestingly enough, the *Odyssey* also has a considerable
revival of the elements of belief that had been so rigorously 'ex-
purgated' from the *Iliad*. The eleventh book, the scene in Hades, is
filled with ghosts and dark blood and eerie noises, like a canvas
of Hieronymus Bosch, not at all heroic in its texture. In the end,
it remained for a poet who stood outside the heroic world to take
the great next step. In the case of Hesiod we are certain, as we
cannot be for the poet of the *Iliad*: it was he who organized the
individual gods into a systematic theogony and made justice into
the central problem of existence, human as well as divine. From
Hesiod a straight line leads to Aeschylus and the other great
tragedians.

In those succeeding centuries the miracle that was Greece
unfolded. Homer having made the gods into men, man learned
to know himself.

Appendix I

THE WORLD OF ODYSSEUS REVISITED*

In March 1957 Bernard Berenson, then in his nineties, wrote as follows to his friend, the Swedish archaeologist Axel Boethius: 'All my life I have been reading about Homer, philological, historical, archaeological, geographical, etc. Now I want to read him as pure art only, as commensurate with the heart and mind while humanity retains both. There appeared recently a book about the *Odyssey* which talked of it as a sociological document only. It had a fabulous success and the American author was at once offered chairs in Oxford as well as Cambridge.'†

Berenson's information was not free from inaccuracy, but his central jibe is a common one and it raises important issues. *The World of Odysseus* has in fact generated much discussion and controversy; the issues transcend the two poems alone, there have been new insights and new information, from comparative study of oral composition, from archaeology, from Near Eastern documents. It is therefore not unreasonable for me to ask, after twenty years, where do I (and the book) stand.

I am a historian; my professional interest in the *Iliad* and *Odyssey* is in their usefulness as tools, as documents, for the study of Bronze Age, Dark Age and archaic Greek history. I see no need to justify in principle that way of looking at the two poems, or of any other poems that have ever been written. But perhaps, after twenty years of experience, some of it rather frustrating, I may be permitted to state a few commonplaces explicitly, in the hope that several familiar red herrings can thereafter be ignored.

* An abridged and slightly revised version of my Presidential Address for 1974 to the Classical Association, published in its *Proceedings*, 71 (1974), pp. 13-31, and reprinted by kind permission of the Association.
† *The Selected Letters of Bernard Berenson*, ed. A. K. McComb (London: Hutchinson), p. 294.

1. I do not suggest that the Homeric poems can be looked at only as sociological documents, or that they cannot be discussed purely as great art, without reference to the historicity of the Trojan War or of the suitors in Ithaca. I have chosen one line of study that suits my purposes and my professional competence. I make no claim for superiority of that line, let alone exclusiveness, but I cannot refrain from noting that the 'pure art' exponents find it very difficult to remain within their competence, to resist sliding from Homeric literary analysis and criticism over to the Trojan War, Hittite treaties, helmets and shields, feudalism and the rest of the non-literary baggage of Homeric scholarship.

2. I accept that the *Iliad* and *Odyssey* are greater poems than any others of their genre. The 12,000 lines which the South Slavic bard Avdo Mededovič once composed to order for Milman Parry are pretty poor stuff, whatever their value as a demonstration of technique. What I do not accept is that such judgements constitute an objection to the comparative analysis of oral composition as a genre, an analysis which is as necessary a preliminary to the historian's use of the poems as to the literary critic's. Does anyone refuse to study Tudor drama as a genre because Shakespeare was so much greater than his fellow-playwrights, or baroque church cantatas because of Bach's towering genius?

3. Greek was the spoken and written language of Mycenaean Greece, Dark Age Greece, archaic, classical and Hellenistic Greece, to go no further. Therefore it is a false method to examine continuity and technique by the common device of dredging up a word, a phrase, an object and parading it as proof of some great discovery. We still ask a lawyer to draw up a last will and testament, centuries after it ceased to be meaningful to employ both the Anglo-Saxon and the Norman French label. There are still men in this country who sign documents (and for all I know address each other) precisely like characters in Shakespeare's historical plays: Norfolk, Leicester, Cambridge. That reveals some level of continuity, no doubt, but the mere fact offers only negligible information about either our society or the society in which such terminology arose. What would really require serious discussion would be the total absence of Mycenaen 'continuities'

in the *Iliad* and *Odyssey*, if that were the case, which of course it is not.

Merely to say that poems are also documents is not saying much. What sort of documents? And, in the particular case of the Homeric poems, documents of and about which historical period, which historical society?

For example, we read in a recent work on the Catalogue of Ships: 'The world depicted in the poems is, after all, essentially a poetic world, not a real world at all, though the material setting is largely realistic: can we really believe that real Greeks ever did behave as the heroes behave? . . . the fondness of the heroes for the giving and receiving of gifts surely does not reflect a society in which gift-giving was an essential part of the economy: the giving and receiving of gifts is rather an integral part of the heroic ideal. The fact that the poems betray little if any knowledge of the quasi-feudal bureaucracy of the tablets may not be so much due to the disappearance of the system as to the fact that it was something quite alien to the poetic tradition, and therefore failed to impinge upon it, however fundamental it may have been to real life.'*

The will to believe or not to believe is not an argument, all the less so when the same authors go on immediately to manifest equal disbelief respecting the Linear B tablets, as unpoetical a collection of texts as one can imagine: 'But in fact one wonders whether the very complexity and comprehensiveness revealed by the Linear B tablets may not be giving a false impression of what life was really like in Mycenaean Greece.' That Homer was a poet, not a historian, hardly needs saying. Nor is it really worth saying unless one is prepared to examine seriously what that implies. The scholars I have just quoted 'really believe' that the Trojan War and the Catalogue of Ships were in essence authentic and historical, not mere products of the brain of the poet. Why? In what respect do they differ from gift-giving in their inherent credibility? I am not aware of any stigmata which brand some components of the tale, and, by their absence, acquit others.

* R. Hope Simpson and J. F. Lazenby, *The Catalogue of Ships in Homer's Iliad* (Oxford, 1970), pp. 8-9.

Homer, we must remind ourselves, was not just a poet, any poet, or any kind of poet, he was an exponent of a particular kind of poetry, oral heroic poetry. Much is now known about the procedures and the rules of oral composition, and what is known cannot be dismissed by fiat when that suits a modern commentator. One rule of oral composition before an audience is that the poem must satisfy the requirement of verisimilitude — I do not say truth — over which the audience exercises extensive control. The poets' insistence that they are narrating truly, for which there is worldwide testimony, reflects this fundamental condition of their art. Of course they invented. Intricate internal analysis of the formulae has shown that neither Patroclus nor the suitors of the *Odyssey* were part of an ancient tradition. But then, the twelve Saracen chieftains of the *Song of Roland* have either Germanic names or blatantly made-up names, and Roland himself may have been a poetic invention — and in this instance the argument is based on contemporary documents, not merely on internal analysis of the poem.

We, alas, have no similar control documents, and we must seek other canons. If we accept that there were limits to poetic invention, have we any tests, not for individual names, incidents or statements, which I believe to be beyond our control, but for categories of people or actions? I shall quickly consider one that I hold to be valid and another, commonly and casually applied, that is logically invalid, at least in the way it is employed.

Fifty years ago the French sociologist Marcel Mauss published his famous account of the integral role of gift-giving in a large range of societies. Twenty years ago I showed that gift-giving in the Homeric poems is consistent, I might even say absolutely consistent, with the analysis made by Mauss (who, curiously, ignored the ancient Greeks in his study). If, as has been said (and I have earlier quoted), the practice 'surely does not reflect a society' but an 'heroic ideal', we are driven to the conclusion that, by a most remarkable intuition, Homer was a predecessor of Marcel Mauss, except that he (or his tradition) invented an institution which nearly three thousand years later Mauss discovered to be a social reality. Nor is that all. Tamil heroic poetry of South India reveals a comparable network of gift-giving and gift-exchange. Not only Homer, then, but other oral composers, in distant lands, were all instinctive, premature Marcel Mausses.

So absurd a conclusion requires no more of our time. The test I am putting forward is the presence in a given body of heroic poetry of a behaviour pattern which can be shown, by comparative study, to have existed in one or another society outside the one under examination. Such a behaviour pattern, if it is integral to the account and reasonably consistent in the portrayal, must be accepted by us as part of a social reality. It cannot be the product of poetic imagination or invention.

Now for the 'test' I propose to reject. Modern Homeric scholarship is normally coy and evasive in its response to the question, What did the poet and his audiences 'really believe' about all the divine capers in the poems, the quarrelling and lovemaking, the nastiness, especially with respect to the unfortunate, even though heroic, mortals? Despite the loud silence, I suspect that a considerable consensus exists, and I take Cedric Whitman as its spokesman. He is at least forthright on the subject:

'Homer certainly did not invent this method of objectifying states into divinities. . . . If one asks wherein Homer's part lay, again it must be sought in the control imposed upon the complex possibilities of the traditional procedure. Like the characters of the *Iliad*, the gods of the *Iliad* are refashioned, within the limits of their assigned spheres, to fit the poem. . . . Such liberty in dealing with the gods was always the rule with Greek poets. . . . As in the dramatists, and especially Sophocles, the gods of Homer are symbolic predicates of action, character, and circumstance. . . . Zeus' arbitrariness and his subservience to "fate", with their apparent contradictions, are actually mere appearances, modes of speaking. The "fate" which he must acknowledge is the poet's scenario viewed as ineluctable fact. . . .'*

That is an application of what I shall call 'the man on the Clapham omnibus' test, once a favourite cliché of English judges for 'the reasonable man'. To the man on the Clapham omnibus, Apollo shooting arrows into the army camp is, if he doesn't think

* *Homer and the Heroic Tradition* (Harvard, 1958), pp. 222-8.

it just silly, a symbolic predicate; or perhaps Apollo's arrows are a fancy poetical synonym for *Bacillus Pasteurella*, the bubonic plague bacillus. But why the man on the Clapham omnibus? Why not the anxious old woman in Euboea who explained during Holy Week, 'Of course I am anxious, for if Christ does not rise tomorrow, we shall have no corn this year.'* What symbolic predicate are we to believe Sophocles to have used to feed the snake of Asclepius which he housed (or was believed to have housed) for a considerable time after its arrival in Athens from Epidaurus?

I do not propose to embark on the thorny subject of Homeric religion. My present concern is solely with modern commentators who blithely permit the poets to play tricks with their gods and their religion, to 'refashion' them as their 'scenario', but who will not permit the poets equal freedom of manoeuvre with, say, the Trojan War. Of course, *we* have no difficulty in accepting the reality of the latter whereas we cannot conceivably accept the happenings on Mount Olympus as anything but symbols or poetic fictions. Our beliefs, however, are not the point at issue but the poet's procedures, his values, his beliefs, the limitations on his right to invent or refashion. Homer's gods 'cannot be treated simply as an "apparatus", . . . or mentally subtracted from the poems without affecting their essence.'†

The historian of ideas and values has no more Satanic seducer to guard against than the man on the Clapham omnibus, heavily supported in our field by something called the 'poetic tradition'. That the latter existed requires no demonstration. Tradition is part of the human condition: we are all enmeshed in a multiplicity of traditions, sophisticated Homeric scholars as well as 'simple' illiterate bards. But tradition is a social phenomenon, not something handed down to the first bard from Mount Olympus on twelve Linear B tablets. If the 'poetic tradition' allows Homer to do something, or prevents him, that requires explanation of the same order, bound by the same demands of metho-

* Quoted from Gilbert Murray's foreword to T. H. Gaster, *Thespis* (New York: Anchor Books, 1961, and Gordian, 1974), p. 10.

† G. S. Kirk, *Myth* (California and Cambridge, 1973), p. 33.

dological rigour, as something Homer is claimed to have done or not done out of his 'own imagination'. Tradition as a sufficient explanation in itself is an evasion of the obligation to explain or understand, as in the example I gave earlier, that Homer's ignorance of the world of the tablets may be attributed 'to the fact that it was something quite alien to the tradition'.

On any view, the tradition behind the *Iliad* and *Odyssey* was neither stationary nor petrified, whether in language or in content. Homer was neither a gramophone record nor a Xerox machine. We must allow ignorance of the distant past as a possible factor in explaining 'omissions', and, though that complicates matters considerably, we must also envisage a mixture of ignorance and imperfect knowledge, as revealed in the deliberate archaisms. Under that heading I include the omission of institutions and practices of the eighth or seventh century known to be, or believed to be, relatively modern. I also include those elements of the tradition, essential to the image of an heroic past, which the poets were incapable of visualizing any longer but which they had somehow to portray.

The great luxurious palaces of the heroes, for example — how are they described? After a century of desperate scholarly attempts to reconstruct from Homer something that could be called, by a great effort of will, a Mycenaean palace, it must be obvious that the attempt was foredoomed. The core of the Homeric palace belongs to the early first millennium B.C., the scale, the intricacy and the massive gold, silver, ivory, and bronze decorations belong to the imagination, as the poets tried, with the help of their inherited formulas, to elevate the pitiful buildings they knew, which they also knew to be inappropriate, to something they could not visualize but imagined to be appropriate. That we now know rather firmly from archaeology. And then there are the famous chariots, employed as taxis not only to transport the heroes to the battle but also to move them about within the mêlée, in which the warriors were armed with a javelin, the wrong weapon for chariot-fighting. The fact of chariot-fighting had survived in the tradition and nothing else, not even the technical vocabulary needed if one wished to describe it (unlike the very precise vocabulary for hand-to-hand combat on foot). So the poets borrowed from two post-Mycenaean and still familiar objects (again known to us from archaeological finds, chiefly vase paintings), namely, the light racing chariot and the cavalryman with his javelin, in order to compose the nonsense we read in the poems about military chariots. This was deliberate archaizing: not once does a mounted horse appear in a battle scene, though riding on horseback is permitted in similes. The parallel with bronze and iron weaponry comes at once to mind.

Iron, as everyone knows, does creep into the poems occasionally (unlike the cavalryman). So does the temple. There is no perfect consistency in the archaizing (or in anything else), no perfect accuracy in the details. That would be too much to ask of the poets; indeed, grave suspicion would arise if there were. An important methodological rule follows: no argument may legitimately be drawn from a single line or passage or usage. Only the patterns, the persistent statements have any standing.

I spoke earlier of 'audience control' over the versimilitude of the poetry, and it is important to appreciate that this aspect of the history of the Greek oral tradition — an aspect which is strictly hypothetical, of course — not only permitted archaizing, but demanded it. The audiences, whoever they may have been, had no more genuine knowledge of the 'once upon a time' world of the heroes than had the poets, but they too knew that it was in essentials unlike their own. Heroes fought in chariots and feasted in great palaces, and so on, and the wildly inaccurate ways in which the poets described these things seemed right. How could they possibly know that they were in fact wrong? In a world wholly without writing, and therefore without records, disagreements could be resolved only by subjective judgements, by reference to the way it had been said before, by the superior *auctoritas* of one poet as against another, by anything other than reference to a document. Whatever dropped out of the poetic repertoire soon disappeared from 'memory' forever; whatever innovation proved 'successful' soon became accepted as part of the tradition ever since once upon a time.

And the formulas, the building blocks of the poems, possessed the necessary flexibility for both moving the substance along with changes in the world itself and, at the same time, restraining it from excessive contemporaneity. The flexibility and continuous evolution of the formulas and the formulaic method are a major discovery resulting from linguistic analysis of the poems in the past two decades. We can now feel confident that formulas were lost, replaced, elaborated; that the process was uneven in tempo, slow and archaizing; that it followed a certain logic. Whereas the diction for the helmet and the shield, two objects intimately connected with 'changes in the technology and practice' of warfare 'is far from settled, less regular for the helmet than for the shield, and least settled where the sense of the description refers to an object from a more recent archaeological period', in contrast 'the diction for the unchanging sea is very settled indeed'.*

Now, it is obvious that important as verisimilitude may be in the relations between poet and audience, it is useless as a test for the historian. The effort to describe and locate the world of Odysseus cannot rest on so weak a support. Nor can the tale of the Trojan War itself be rescued, as is often attempted, by an appeal to the fact that it was credible to generations and centuries of poets and their listeners or readers. Siegfried, the twelve Saracen chieftains at Roncevaux, King Arthur, even Brute the Trojan have all passed that test *summa cum laude*. The historian wishing to make use of the *Iliad* and *Odyssey* as documents must make some basic discrimination. He may not, though that is the normal practice, jumble together the various products of human behaviour. I shall examine in turn four different categories: manufactured objects, the narrative (including the *dramatis personae*), institutions and values.

It is embarrassing to discuss material objects, but unavoidable. Since Schliemann found Troy a century ago, incalculable energy has been expended (and still is) in correlating archaeological finds with the poems, largely in the effort to demonstrate the authenticity of Homer's Mycenaean world. And what a stony field was being ploughed, producing a pitiful crop — the boar's

* J. B. Hainsworth, *The Flexibility of the Homeric Formula* (Oxford, 1968), pp. 113-14.

tusk helmet, Ajax's body-shield, Nestor's cup, perhaps two or three other items which archaeology has authenticated, and the existence of palaces and war-chariots (without a shred of accurate knowledge about either). On this question of dating, of which period is represented in the poems, objects have evidentiary value only if they have a fixed duration; in the case of the presumed Mycenaean base of the poems, only objects that can be shown to have become obsolete, to have disappeared, in other words, with the collapse of the Mycenaean world. And in the end, the result of all this past effort has been merely to demonstrate that formulaic, presumably oral, poetry was already being composed in the Bronze Age, and that bits of it, tiny bits in an occasional phrase or verse, managed to survive down to Homer.

We need not dispute that conclusion, nor do we need to go on seeking further proof for a proposition so obvious and unilluminating. But there are two unacceptable corollaries that scholars continue to draw. One is that these bits of Mycenaean survival are for some mysterious reason more weighty than the whole mass of material which is either garbled Mycenaean or demonstrably post-Mycenaean or at the least both Mycenaean and post-Mycenaean. The other is that Schliemann's discovery in the shaft-graves of Mycenae of a cup that looks enough like (though not identical with) Nestor's cup argues in favour of the existence of a historical King Nestor, reigning in Pylos more or less in the way the poems suggest. Probably no one states the methodological argument in such an exposed way, but it is no less illogical for being left unexpressed.

As for the narrative, even if one concedes that any particular event or person may be authentic, or at least have an authentic prototype, one has achieved nothing because there is no key with which to distinguish the historical from the fictitious. The absence of documentary control I have already stressed embraces, with respect to the narrative, an absence of external documentation, among the neighbours of the Greeks who retained their literacy and kept records of one sort or another. The most massive, most learned and most ingenious attempt ever made to overcome this recognized weakness in our knowledge failed at the critical point:

neither Troy nor mainland Greece appears in the Hittite texts on which the attempt was primarily based. That leaves us with a *Hamlet* not only without the Prince of Denmark but also without Denmark. Nor can it be reiterated often enough that the excavations at Hissarlik have not produced a jot of evidence to support the tales.*

However, let us not press too hard; let us be content with the view, which commands sufficient support among specialists, that Troy VIIa fell in the last third of the thirteenth century B.C. The implications for the Homeric narrative do not appear to have attracted serious enough attention. Those who believe that the *Iliad* and *Odyssey* have roots stretching well back into the Mycenaean period must explain how that tradition became so concentrated round an event which occurred, at best, one generation earlier. Thucydides, we know, foresaw in 431 B.C. that the war which had broken out between Athens and Sparta would be the greatest war of all time, greater even than the Trojan War, and he dedicated his life to its history as it unfolded. Are we to assume that an unknown thirteenth-century bard had the same insight when the Achaean expedition sailed from Aulis?

Those who accept the Trojan War as historical, it seems to me, have no alternative but to accept that the narrative we have is a Dark Age, not a Mycenaean, tradition. If there were already a tradition of heroic poetry, around other, earlier wars and battles, there would not be the slightest difficulty for the bards in making the shift. 'The things that can happen in battle are . . . limited, and the descriptions of them, within an oral formulaic convention that does not encourage variegated or introspective analysis are even more so. Thus two heroes, one from each side, meet in the mêlée of battle; they utter threats and boasts; if in chariots, they dismount; one of them hurls a spear, which usually misses; the other reciprocates', and so on.† The heroes themselves, recognizable individuals though a few of them may be, are as a group an aggregate of types. Hence Patroclus could be introduced into the story at a very late date, and for nearly two

* See Appendix II.
† G. S. Kirk, *The Songs of Homer* (Cambridge, 1962), p. 75.

thousand years no one noticed that he was a fictitious interloper. Hence, too, a wholly or largely fictitious, or a totally distorted, Trojan War could have grown up in the early Dark Age without being scarred all over by tell-tale signs of the falsity of the narrative.

That leaves social institutions and social values, which may be considered together. A model can be constructed, imperfect, incomplete, untidy, yet tying together the fundamentals of political and social structure with an appropriate value system in a way that stands up to comparative analysis, the only control available to us in the absence of external documentation. When I say that I still hold to the model of *The World of Odysseus*, I do not claim that I made no mistakes, or that I have not changed my mind in twenty years. In a new edition of the book, I shall not only make changes and adjustments in the light of all the new research, but I shall also reconsider at least one section radically, that devoted to the lower classes and their status.* But I stand by the model as a whole, and I also retain the conclusion that it is a picture of the early Dark Age, the tenth and ninth centuries B.C., distorted here and there by misunderstandings and by anachronisms.

My original reference to the presence of anachronisms has greatly irritated some critics. I do not understand why. Are we not all familiar with the inability of historical novelists and film producers, despite all their research, their technical advisers and their copy editors, to eliminate an occasional false note, usually contemporary? What else could one possibly expect of oral poets? The critical point is rather that the model is so coherent, and this also rules out the common statement that what we find in the poems is either a fiction (which I have already dealt with) or a composite drawn from different eras. Given the profound differences between the Bronze Age and the eighth century B.C., such a composite would be blatantly artificial, unable to withstand careful social analysis.

This question of the location in time of the world of Odysseus

* As I have indicated in the Preface of this new edition, in the end I found no alternative formulation beyond a slight change in nuance in the wording.

is so important that I must consider the objections and the new insights that have accumulated since I first proposed an early Dark Age date. The choice lies between that period and the poet's own time, now that the ground beneath a supposed Mycenaean world of Odysseus has been removed by the Linear B tablets, assisted by continuous archaeological excavation and study.

Elimination of the poet's own world, say the mid-eighth century, is handicapped by two difficulties. The first is that we know so little about it: the argument therefore tends to be circular if it is held that the *Iliad* and *Odyssey* reflect that world substantially. The second is that many aspects of life did not change very much from the tenth century to the eighth, or even from the Bronze Age to the eighth century. No matter how radically land tenure may have been transformed, for example, the pursuits of agriculture and pasturage, the cycle of the seasons, the ploughing and sowing and harvesting, the struggle with blight and marauding animals would have been relatively unaffected.

It is therefore impossible to make as much of the similes as has become habitual. We may take it as generally accepted that the developed Homeric similes are characterized by linguistic lateness and were probably composed at a late date. It is in the similes, furthermore, that we find the 'unheroic' side of the heroic world. But is 'unheroic' also necessarily contemporary? 'We can safely detect the world of the eighth century', writes A. M. Snodgrass in closing the best book we have on the Dark Age, 'in the more homely images of hunting deer, wild goat and boar; of fishing and diving for oysters; of horse riding and ivory horse-trappings; of ploughing, reaping, winnowing, milling, irrigation and other activities linked with arable farming; of vine-growing; of tree-felling and ship-building; of stock-breeding, tanning and working in wool; of fairly advanced metallurgy in gold and silver as well as iron; and of trading by sea.'* Safely? Were there no hunting, ploughing, working in wool, trading by sea and so on right through the list in the tenth century, or the fifteenth? What is there in the similes that says this is eighth-century winnowing,

* *The Dark Age of Greece* (Edinburgh, 1971), p. 435.

not ninth? Are we to draw some conclusion about eighth-century society from the fact that only once (8.527-30) is a simile based on a family relationship other than that between parent and child? Or from the fact that the largest number of similes turn to nature and the elements, not to man and his doings?

Nothing, perhaps, exposes the lack of rigour, the absence of method, than the response to the lion similes. Snodgrass rules them out; they are 'more likely to derive from Bronze Age tradition than from the new accessibility of the regions to the east where lions were still common'; more likely, he says, 'on several grounds' which he does not state. Others, on the contrary, argue that the absence of lion-*hunting* proves that the poet drew on contemporary knowledge. I know no way to choose between the two views, both of which neglect the well-known importance of the lion in Near Eastern cultures stretching a long way back. If the Etruscans could derive their passion for lions from Near Eastern sources, I can see no reason why the Greeks could not have done the same — at any time. Need I recall the gate at Mycenae?

In the final analysis, I do not really mind what view one takes about the contemporaneity or non-contemporaneity of the similes because they are wholly uninformative. Even without them we should have known that men winnowed and hunted and raised stock in Homer's own world, and with them we know nothing more. But there comes a point when I begin to mind very much. That point is reached when Snodgrass continues his final remarks with 'Homer's recognition of the great social and political advance of his day, the rise of the *polis*', a recognition revealed in 'walls, docks, temples and a market-place; . . . the technical building-knowledge . . . of contemporary constructions' and the fact that the nobles lived in the town rather than on their estates. Apart from the last item, the residential pattern, which applies to any period in Greek history from the early Bronze Age on, this is a perfect example of the confusion between objects and institutions. Even as an external portrait, furthermore, the Homeric city is utterly 'faceless', most obviously in Scheria, the town of the Phaeacians; not a word is said about its residential quarters, streets or terraces of houses. Yet the latter is the outstanding element of the contemporary city we know best archaeologically, Old Smyrna, which claimed Homer as its native son. And of the political or social institutions of the real Old Smyrna we learn next to nothing from the physical remains.

Scheria is critical for the argument. It has become a commonplace to cite Scheria as a reflection of the Greek western colonization movement contemporary with Homer, in particular to quote the opening lines of the sixth book of the *Odyssey*. 'Godlike' Nausithous, we read, removed his people from their native Hyperia, where they were under constant attack by the Cyclopes, drew a wall round the new settlement, Scheria, built houses and temples, and divided the arable. These four verses could equally reflect the first Greek settlements in Ionia about or soon after 1000 B.C.; only those who continue to play the idle game of plotting Odysseus's travels on a map of the western Mediterranean need to locate Scheria in the west. Let us concede that, however, and even concede the 'colonization' reality behind the four verses. We then have no more than an unimportant anachronism. What matters about the Phaeacians, about that whole lengthy episode in the *Odyssey*, is their unreality, their position halfway between the world of fantasy Odysseus was finally leaving and the real world to which he was soon to return. Magical ships that powered themselves were not instruments of the westward colonization, nor did magic gardens await the migrants on arrival. In so far as there is identifiable reality in Phaeacia, it is the monarchy, not substantially different in structure (though very different in tone) from the monarchy in Ithaca. There is nothing in Phaeacia apart from the four verses, that resembles eighth-century Ischia or Cumae, Syracuse, Leontini or Megara Hyblaea. It is equally impossible to find the mother-cities, Chalcis, Corinth, Megara, in the poems; that is to say, the social organization of the world of Odysseus was inadequate for the tasks we know some *poleis* contemporary with Homer to have performed.

After these negative arguments, it remains to consider whether there are positive grounds for an early Dark Age location of the world of Odysseus. Snodgrass, for one, concludes with a firm denial. However, the sole basis I can find in the book for his 'personal conviction' is the material poverty of the early Dark Age, and that seems to me to involve a serious misunderstanding. The poets were clearly dominated by the belief that they were describing a lost golden age; hence they magnified the scale as best they could, usually very inaccurately for reasons I have already examined, but the falsity of scale and the misdirection of the imagination do not in themselves falsify the institutional core. Gift-exchange, which is Snodgrass' specific example, can operate in the most elaborate way with cowrie shells. A low standard of life is irrelevant outside the obsessional concentration on material objects.

The weakness of archaeological argument in this particular context is that too many of the objects had a continuous existence (as types) from the early Dark Age into the archaic age (and even later). Is 'personal conviction' then the only test? I believe not, and I shall risk disputing the experts from four groups of evidence.

The first consists of the bronze tripods and 'glittering cauldrons' which are noticeably prominent in the Homeric image of treasure. Although such objects are known from the Late Bronze Age, they were so marginal in that period as to impose the conclusion that here we have a certain Dark Age element, well attested in excavations, especially (but not solely) at Olympia and other shrines. The exact dating of many finds is still under discussion, as is the question of whether or not the original impetus came from the eastern Mediterranean. It is undisputed, however, that the cauldron and tripod found in a Fortetsa grave at Cnossus (along with a small lead figurine of a lion, I note) date from the tenth century, and that further evidence from the early Dark Age continues to come to light.

Clearly no decision about the date of the world of Odysseus can rest on the tripods and cauldrons, but the case improves when we turn, second, to domestic architecture. Again we are faced with a continuous Dark Age production, but in this instance one in which there was also continuous development, fairly well understood now and even, within limits, capable of being set against the reality underlying the imaginative Homeric descriptions. The most systematic inquiry concludes that 'in its architecture and its function, the house of Odysseus is untouched by the most recent trends which were to make a breakthrough in the period that followed'.* If this is a correct conclusion — I have no independent judgement on the subject — it must mean that the architecture in the poems received its main outlines not at the time of Homer but in earlier generations.

My third and fourth categories do not consist of objects, but their assessment rests on material remains. I refer to the Phoenician monopoly of trade and to cremation of the dead. In real life the former reflects the period before 800 B.C. By that date the presence of Greek traders in the Levant is firmly attested, and there is no trace of them in Homer. We are thus moving to a firmer foundation for an early Dark Age society, and the practice of cremation then provides considerable acceleration. Save for one ambiguous passage (IV 174-77), whenever Homer reports the disposal of the dead, it is always and only by cremation. The Mycenaean world buried its dead, with negligible exceptions; by about 1050 B.C. cremation of adults became the rule in most of the Greek world; by 850 or 800 inhumation made a substantial, though not complete, recovery. Anyone who has no 'phenomena to save' will naturally conclude that Homer was reflecting a post-Mycenaean, pre-contemporary practice.

* H. Drerup, *Griechische Baukunst in geometrischer Zeit* [*Archaeologia Homerica* II, chap. O (Göttingen, 1969)], p. 133.

SCHLIEMANN'S TROY—ONE HUNDRED YEARS AFTER*

In a report on his first excavation of Hissarlik, written on May 24, 1873, for the *Augsburger Allgemeine Zeitung*, Schliemann announced categorically: 'Since I consider my task to be fully accomplished, on 15th June of this year I shall bring the excavations here in Troy to an end for ever.' Nevertheless, five years later he was digging there again, and on New Year's Day 1880 he wrote to Harper's asking them to take on the American publication of his *Ilios*: 'No money and no pain has been spared to make this work settle and exhaust for ever the Trojan question.'† That 'for ever' had an even shorter run, a mere two years. On April 15, 1883, following his third excavation, he offered his *Troja* to another American publisher, Scribner's: 'I have now terminated for ever the excavations on the site of sacred Ilion. . . . This book will contain an account of the most important discoveries I ever made in my life and it will settle the Trojan question definitely for ever. . . . Troy is now entirely excavated. . . .'‡

That proved to be a seven-year 'for ever'. The fourth excavation, in 1890, lasted for five months and produced the sensational discovery that Troy II, the city of the great treasure, far from being Priam's Troy, as Schliemann and all his followers had firmly believed, was very much older. Priam and the Trojan War had to be shifted to the level Schliemann had previously

---

* An abridged and slightly revised version of the Mortimer Wheeler Archaeological Lecture delivered at the British Academy on November 20, 1974, and published in its *Proceedings*, 60 (1974), pp. 393-412.

Copyright © by the British Academy and reprinted by kind permission.

† Schliemann corresponded in several languages. When the original was in English, as in this instance, I have quoted verbatim. I shall not indicate the language of the original in subsequent quotations.

‡ Quotations from Schliemann's letters are from his *Briefwechsel*, ed. E. Meyer (2 vols., Berlin 1953-58) or from the letters to Max Müller published in the *Journal of Hellenic Studies*, 82 (1962), pp. 75-105.

labelled 'Lydian', but now simply Troy VI. Schliemann died before the planned 1891 campaign, and it was 1893 before Dörpfeld could continue their joint work, which he completed the following year. Dörpfeld lived to help the Cincinnati team, who excavated for seven seasons between 1932 and 1938. By then, in truth, Troy was entirely excavated.

The final reports of the Cincinnati mission began to appear in 1950. In the fourth volume, published in 1958, which dealt with the relevant stratum, now known as Troy VIIa, Blegen felt able to write that the 'fundamental historicity of the Greek tradition', its 'basic solidity and reliability . . . can no longer be denied'. Five years later, in a popular account, he expanded that lapidary pronouncement: 'It can no longer be doubted, when one surveys the state of our knowledge today, that there really was an actual historical Trojan War in which a coalition of Achaeans, or Mycenaeans, under a king whose overlordship was recognized, fought against the people of Troy and their allies.'*

I was not the only one whose capacity to doubt had not been destroyed quite so totally. What evidence, I and others asked, did you find, or did Schliemann or Dörpfeld find, in all the years of excavation at Hissarlik that points to a coalition of Achaeans or Mycenaeans under a king whose overlordship was recognized? So far as I can discover, the answer is limited to a single bronze arrowhead found in Street 710 of Troy VIIa. Furthermore, how did Blegen provide a fixed point in time, by archaeological evidence? The answer turns out to be unstable and unsatisfactory. The dates rest, of necessity, on the pottery remains and on nothing else. In the 1958 report Blegen wrote that Troy VIIa was short-lived, that its duration cannot be determined 'precisely', that 'a century or less, possibly even within a generation of men', seemed plausible, a generation which he then tried to narrow to the period *c.* 1275-1240 B.C. But in the later popular book he had Troy VIIa destroyed about 1250 B.C. 'if not a decade or two earlier' on one page, and three pages later, 'about 1260 B.C., if not indeed somewhat earlier'. Blegen was obviously motivated

---

* C. W. Blegen *et al.*, *Troy*, iv (Princeton, 1958), p. 10, and Blegen, *Troy and the Trojans* (London, 1963), p. 20, respectively.

/ reasons extraneous to his own archaeological evidence and judgement, namely, the wish to get Troy destroyed well before the destruction of Pylos. When I commented on the chronoolgical instability of the 'undeniable' Trojan War, J. L. Caskey, who was most closely associated with Blegen in both the excavations and the publication, replied that we 'as yet must allow a latitude of some twenty or thirty years toward the end of the thirteenth century' for the date of the destruction of VIIa.* By no arithmetic known to me can 'a generation of men' be dated within those widely separated end-points, nor is 1260 or 1250 or even 1240 a date that one would normally identify as falling within 'a latitude of some twenty or thirty years towards the end of the thirteenth century'.

Nor does that exhaust our chronological difficulties. Troy VIIa had two architectural peculiarities: the houses, of poor quality and small in size, were huddled in terraces, and the familiar large storage jars were sunk to the rims into the floors of the dwellings and covered with stone slabs so that they could be walked over. 'We may, with some degree of confidence,' writes Blegen, 'recognize the endeavour of the threatened community to lay up sufficient supplies of food and drink to withstand a siege.' Homer, everyone knows, stretched the siege of Troy into a ten-year operation but neglected to allow for Achaean replacements or supplies. Are we now asked to believe that for thirty-five years, and perhaps longer, the Trojans anticipated that siege, that when they resettled the city after the destruction of Troy VI by a violent earthquake, they said to themselves, 'One day the Achaeans will come under a recognized overlord; so let us prepare by huddling together and sinking *pithoi* into the floors, in which we shall be able to store food and drink when the evil day arrives'?

Just a century earlier, on October 18, 1873, Schliemann wrote to the sceptical Max Müller, with the directness that characterized his correspondence and his books and articles: 'It was . . . beyond any doubt the treasure of the last king, of the king who reigned when the catastrophe happened and this king being

* *Journal of Hellenic Studies*, 84 (1964), p. 10.

called Priamos by Homer I call the treasure Priam's treasure and *have no other evidence of the correctness of the name*' (my italics). In one respect, then, 'Schliemann's Troy' remains unchanged one hundred years after. The archaeology is vastly improved in technique and the quantity of the documentation is incalculably increased, but the central question is being answered in exactly the same way and almost exactly the same language, though perhaps less 'naïvely'. I believe this to be a unique situation in the history of modern archaeology; not even Camelot can touch it.

Schliemann began his twenty-two year career as a working archaeologist with the firm conviction that not only was Homer in the *Iliad* to be read as if he were a reliable 'war correspondent', but that the *Odyssey* was a mixture of ordnance survey and logbook. So in a few days' scratching in Ithaca in 1868 he located the farm of Laërtes, the field where Eumaeus lived and the 'cyclopean ruins' of ten of his pigsties, he found cremation urns which 'very possibly . . . preserved the ashes of Odysseus and Penelope or their descendants', and he dug unsuccessfully for the roots of the olive tree from the wood of which Odysseus constructed his marriage-bed.* His rapid publication in book form of such discoveries did not meet a warm reception. Tozer, the leading authority on ancient geography, suggested in a short review that 'a little more criticism might have saved him a good deal of trouble'.†

Not many years were to go by before Schliemann himself would have agreed. In August 1873 we find him writing to Charles Newton, a few months after his discovery of the great treasure in Troy II, a stratum which was flat and without an acropolis: 'Homer is an epic poet and no historian. He saw neither the great tower of Ilium, nor the divine wall, or Priam's Palace because when he visited Troy 300 years after its destruction all those monuments were for 300 years couched with its 10-feet thick layers of the red ashes and ruins of Troy. . . . Homer made *no* excavations to bring those monuments to light,

* *Ithaka, der Peloponnes und Troja*, ed. E. Meyer (Darmstadt, 1973). pp. 39, 51-2, 31, and 28-9, respectively.
† *The Academy*, 1 (1869), p. 22.

. . . Ancient Troy has no Akropolis and the Pergamos is a pure invention of the poet.'

Such a rapid about-face represents an aspect of Schliemann's temperament that is perhaps less well known and merits a little of our attention. It is, I believe, as important in his work as the more familiar and often tempestuous irascibility. The latter can be documented endlessly. I shall restrict myself to one example, which I have chosen because it involves Frank Calvert, the American consul in the Dardanelles who offered Schliemann free rights to dig on the half of the mound of Hissarlik which he personally owned, helped him throughout his career with the endlessly troublesome Turkish authorities and in many other ways, and after Schliemann's death, was equally helpful to Dörpfeld, as the latter warmly acknowledged. The published correspondence includes a number of quarrelsome letters to, or about, Calvert, but no other reaches the flights of an enormous letter written from Athens in February 1878 to Max Müller in Oxford. I quote an extract:

'I have to point out to you a libel in Frasers Magazine for February written by Wm C. Borlase, President of the Royal Institution of Cornwall and entitled "A Visit to Dr Schliemann's Troy", which for the number of its inculpations and the vehemence of its attacks leaves far behind it any libel that has been written against me before. First of all I must tell you that I have in the Troade a foul fiend of the name of Frank Calvert, who has given the text as well to the libel of Mr Gallenga as to that of Wm Simpson in Frasers Mag. of July last and to the libel now before us. That Calvert has been libelling me for years; I answered him in the *Guardian* three times, showing by my last answer that he is of bad faith and a liar, and therefore his further libels were refused by the Press. But, never daunted, he now enrages the English travellers against me by his ill representation and explication of the ruins of Hissarlik and persuades them to attack me.'

I must leave it to the psychologists to consider whether Schliemann's demonic qualities, of which this letter represents only one side, were not essential, whether he could have achieved what he did without them. My immediate concern is with something else about the man, which I am certain was at least as integral to his career. He retained to the end of his life a sense of inadequacy because of his lack of formal education, and there is genuine pathos in his innumerable appeals for assistance and advice, and in his expressions of gratitude. His letters to Bismarck and the Kaiser may grate, but that is a different matter. No one can fail to be touched by his relations with Virchow, with Müller, with Dörpfeld, with Sayce, Mahaffy, and a host of other scholars. And, what is decisive, he accepted advice on scholarly matters, and he could admit error. It was no small thing, after all, to appreciate almost instantaneously in 1890, at the age of sixty-eight, that Troy II, the Troy of the great treasure, was apparently not Priam's Troy, a view on which he had staked everything for so long.

Having quickly discarded, as we have seen, the Homer-the-war-correspondent prop (though he could never bring himself to abandon it totally when there was a glimmer of a chance to revive it), Schliemann held fast to two other supports. The first was the treasure. As he wrote to Newton in the letter I have already quoted, 'But my treasure shows that Troy was . . . immensely rich, and being rich it was powerful, had many subjects, large dominions. . . .' Confirmation came soon after when he discovered more treasure in the shaft-graves at Mycenae. And the second prop was the topography of the Troad. Homer could not have seen buried Troy, but he could, and did, see the plain of Troy, and he described it with remarkable accuracy.

Then came 1890 and Dörpfeld's excavations of 1893 and 1894, which removed the treasure from the story. Troy VIIa was a pitiful poverty-stricken little place, with no treasure, without even any large and imposing buildings, with nothing remotely resembling a palace. The inhabitants of those remains were not, in Blegen's words, 'made up of the highest grades of society'. Happily, as he immediately goes on to say, the 'houses of the ruling class and of the well-to-do presumably stood on the upper ringed terraces in the central part of the site, whence they were removed without leaving a trace when the top of the hill was shaved off in Hellenistic and Roman times'. Since there is nothing to be done with buildings that have been removed without leaving a trace, apart from presuming their existence, the post-Schliemann generation was left with only the historical topography.

In 1785 Lechevalier identified a 'citadel' outside Bunarbashi, a village some ten kilometres south-east of Hissarlik and correspondingly further from the sea as Homer's Troy, and his identification won majority support despite scattered opposition. Von Hahn's excavation there is 1863 drew a blank, and four years later Schliemann, fresh from his 'discoveries' on Ithaca, satisfied himself that Bunarbashi could not be Troy, partly by 'Homer-the-war-correspondent' arguments but also by the unanswerable argument that trial trenches which he rapidly dug showed no signs of any prehistoric habitation, a conclusion which all subsequent excavations have confirmed. But unanswerable arguments are not necessarily persuasive. I cannot explain the magnetism of the Bunarbashi-Troy equation, for which there was never any good reason, but the fact is that neither Schliemann's work there nor his first excavations at Hissarlik persuaded enough of the archaeologists and philologists, and Schliemann responded to their deafness with his characteristic energy and anger.

That brings me to a puzzle. Schliemann was deeply and persistently upset by the resistance to his discoveries in German classical circles, and he seized on every hint of support, even though some of it was of the lunatic variety. Lunacy was not restricted to one side of the debate. In 1883 a German artillery officer, Ernst Bötticher, began a stream of publications in which he charged Schliemann (and Dörpfeld) with deliberately falsifying their reports in order to conceal that Hissarlik was nothing but a vast ancient crematorium. Schliemann was enraged, rejected the pleas of his friends to ignore the man, and in 1889 brought Bötticher to Hissarlik at his own expense — to no avail. So the following year, 1890, again at his own expense, he organized an international commission of experts, who met at Hissarlik and on March 30 unanimously issued a formal 'protocol' dismissing Bötticher's accusations and claims. Among them were von Duhn,

Carl Humann, Charles Waldstein, and of course Virchow and Frank Calvert.

Characteristically, Bötticher's manic assaults drove Schliemann back to Troy, which he had left for ever, and to the fateful excavation of 1890. But I must revert to my puzzle: why did he not turn to his most obvious allies in Germany, the ancient historians? They, unlike the archaeologists and philologists, had promptly sided with him in dismissing Bunarbashi. In 1877, a year before Schliemann's second period at Hissarlik, there was published in Leipzig a 112-page *Geschichte von Troas*, based on personal autopsy of the site, massive knowledge of the ancient sources, and critical appreciation of Schliemann's publications. The conclusions on the points that concern us were firmly on Schliemann's side: he had settled the Bunarbashi-Hissarlik dispute (though the caustic comment was made that one cannot understand the site from Schliemann's writings alone); there was a historical kernel to the tales of the Trojan War, but we can do nothing with them; that Priam's Troy of the *Iliad* never existed was *proved* by Schliemann's work (then, we must remember, dominated by a wholly false chronology). The author of this book was a young man of twenty-two. His name was Eduard Meyer. A child prodigy, he had become interested in Asia Minor as a schoolboy in Hamburg, embarked on his history of the Troad while a student at Leipzig but put it aside until he could find the opportunity to visit the region. That came when he was appointed tutor in the household of Sir Philip Francis, British consul in Constantinople. In September 1875 Meyer spent six days in the Troad under the guidance of Frank Calvert, and then completed his book. Yet I can find no reference to it in any of Schliemann's published correspondence.

A twenty-two-year-old budding scholar may have seemed too weak a prop, but by the time Schliemann organized his commission to crush Bötticher in 1890, Meyer was Professor of Ancient History in Halle, having previously held the chair in Breslau and published the first volume of his great *Geschichte des Altertums* (*History of Antiquity*). I must confess my inability to explain the puzzle satisfactorily. The reason cannot lie in the rejection by the historians of Schliemann's faith in the Homeric Trojan War or in their lack of enthusiasm for his greater flights of fancy. They were rock-solid on what mattered to Schliemann most, Hissarlik, and Eduard Meyer, at least, was more willing to accept a historical kernel in the tales than was Max Müller, with whom Schliemann maintained the closest relations. It appears that philologists, politicians, engineers, and architects have a measure of *auctoritas* on archaeological matters, but not historians, and in that respect, too, Schliemann's Troy remains unchanged after one hundred years.

A problem in logic now arises. How was it that Schliemann and Meyer came to diametrically opposed judgements of what Schliemann had *proved*, though they agreed on what he had found? This is no mere antiquarian question, for one can replace the two names by contemporary ones, Schliemann by Blegen in particular. The stratification of Troy, the architecture and the pottery, and so on, are as settled in all essentials as they are ever likely to be. But these were not what Schliemann set out to discover. He was after something far greater, the truth about an ancient and famous historical question. And that is still the central question, one hundred years later, to which I shall now devote myself. What do we know about the Trojan War and its background that was not, and could not be, known a century ago before Schliemann and his successors excavated Hissarlik down to virgin soil? First, however, I want briefly to run through five points on which there can be no serious disagreement, outside the lunatic fringe that has always infested this subject. I do so in order to clear the ground of marginal or no longer debatable questions.

1. Schliemann was epithet-prone and still is: from one recent article I have culled the following — 'pseudo-truth', 'fantasy-life', 'clever fraud', 'vulgar', 'dilettante', 'lack of conscience', 'psychopathy', 'egoistic, romantic, tortured, infantile.'* No doubt, but

---

* W. M. Calder III, 'Schliemann on Schliemann: a Study in the Use of Sources', *Greek, Roman and Byzantine Studies*, 13 (1972), pp. 335-53. This article is an important exposé of the hagiography that is current in the guise of biography of Schliemann.

Schliemann was also the father of Greek prehistoric archaeology he is usually acclaimed to have been. He may, as has been said, have dug a site as if he were digging potatoes, but he was also the first man in this field, and virtually in any field of archaeology, to stress stratigraphy and the primacy of pottery for relative chronology. He also appreciated—the significance of which is not often acknowledged—that the highest aim of archaeology is to answer questions. When offered Chiusi as a site in 1875, he refused. 'There are no problems to be resolved', he wrote, 'and I shall not be able to find anything that every museum does not already possess.' His judgement may have been right or it may have been wrong, but the sentiment was impeccably correct.

2. Ancient Troy was at Hissarlik, as virtually the whole of antiquity believed, from Homer on, and the Troy which was besieged and captured by the Achaeans, *if there was a Trojan War*, was the city we now call Troy VIIa, violently destroyed late in the thirteenth century B.C.

3. The poet or poets we call Homer came at the end of a long oral tradition. Schliemann was firm on that, and virtually everyone else who has discussed the 'Homeric problem' since his time. We have a far clearer grasp today of the mechanism of oral poetry and its transmission, thanks to Milman Parry and his successors, but that new—I might say 'revolutionary'—knowledge has made little difference to the question with which I am concerned today.

4. Because of the oral tradition, and because the *Iliad* and *Odyssey* were neither histories nor war correspondents' reports, errors in scale and in the details are to be expected and do not constitute significant arguments, one way or the other, about the essential historicity of the account of the Trojan War. Granting that, I wish the 'other side' would abandon their dance of triumph on such rare occasions as the discovery that a boar's tusk helmet, mentioned once in the *Iliad*, actually existed in Mycenaean Greece. Who has ever pretended that every single word in the *Iliad*, every object, every description of the sea or a hill or a river in the Troad, is as imaginary as the mermaids and the abode of the gods? It becomes ludicrous when Schliemann, Schuchhardt,

Dörpfeld, and countless others seriously hold up as powerful evidence in support of the identification of Hissarlik with Troy the long closing scene in the *Iliad*: Priam is driven by Hermes in a chariot to the Achaean camp, arrives in time to drink and sup with Achilles, gets up in the night and, still accompanied by Hermes, drives with Hector's corpse to the Scamander River, where the god leaves him as he continues to Troy, arriving with the dawn. The distance of this round trip from Hissarlik to the Achaean camp and back is roughly the same as that from the Royal Academy to Tower Hill and back. Even without the help of a god, they could have managed Bunarbashi as well as Hissarlik in that time span.

5. Although it is almost embarrassing to do so, long experience compels me to say explicitly that I accept the proposition that the historical and archaeological problems which exercise us have no great relevance to the literary merits of the poems, or to their entertainment value. In return, I must insist that the literary merits have no relevance to matters of historicity.

And now I return to the central question. In his struggle to obtain official Turkish permission to launch his first excavation in 1871, Schliemann wrote repeatedly, in one form of words or another, that he had 'the purely scientific aim of showing that the Trojan War was not a fable, that Troy and the Pergamos of Priam existed in reality'. Did he succeed? Do the ruins of Troy confirm the historicity of the war which Homer recalled and in part recounted? We know Schliemann's affirmative answer, repeated by Dörpfeld after him and by Blegen still later, by the three men, in other words, who were responsible for this undeniable (and undeniably great) archaeological triumph. Blegen's exact words bear repetition: 'It can no longer be doubted ... that there really was an actual historical Trojan War in which a coalition of Achaeans, or Mycenaeans, under a king whose overlordship was recognized, fought against the people of Troy and their allies.' Blegen then went further. From Troy he moved on to Pylos, and the final reports on that excavation were not called simply *Pylos*, as the earlier ones had been simply *Troy*, but *The Palace of Nestor at Pylos*.

Yet the plain fact is that Blegen found nothing, literally nothing, at either place to warrant his *historical* conclusion. Not a scrap was uncovered at Troy to point to Agamemnon or any other conquering king or overlord, or to a Mycenaean coalition or even to a war. For that blunt assertion I have the highest, if reluctant, authority, that of Caskey, who wrote: 'the physical remains of Troy VIIa do not prove beyond question that the place was captured at all. An accidental fire, in unlucky circumstances, on a day a strong wind was blowing, might account for the general destruction that is known to have occurred. Furthermore, if this citadel was not sacked—and indeed if it was not sacked by Greeks under Agamemnon—we are left without a compelling reason even to go on calling it Troy.'* The 'if' clause is, of course, what the archaeologists have sought to demonstrate, and they have now turned it into a premise.

Normally, material evidence without documents cannot answer the question Schliemann first posed. The most that can legitimately be said one hundred years after Schliemann is that, if there was a Trojan War at all like the Homeric one, Hissarlik is the sole fortress in that part of Asia Minor which could have been under siege, and Troy VIIa is the one stratum which could have been relevant. That is something no doubt—at least we hear no more of Bunarbashi—but it is not much. And there is a fundamental sense in which the intensive and increasingly sophisticated archaeology of the past hundred years has made the position worse, that is to say, it has reduced, rather than increased, the possibility of finding an answer to the key question without the discovery of new documents, in Hittite, for example.

This paradox, that the more we know the worse off we are, deserves further consideration, and chronology offers a good test. Homer of course provides no chronological foundation whatever, nor do the ancient chronographers from Herodotus to Eusebius, since they perforce made their calculations from oral traditions, which, it has now been demonstrated beyond rational disagreement, are invariably misleading in chronological matters. Not every tradition is as distorted as that of the *Nibelungenlied*, which

* *Journal of Hellenic Studies*, 84 (1964), p. 9.

manages to combine into a single complex of events the Ostrogoth Theoderic, who ruled most of the western Empire from 493 to 526, Attila the Hun, who invaded Italy in 452 and died in 453, forty years before the accession of Theoderic, and a certain Pilgrim, who was bishop of Passow from 971 to 979. But for the historian a 100-year error is not significantly less vicious than a 400-year error. There are those among us, I concede, who insist that, or at least behave as if, the Greeks by some mysterious process performed chronological miracles in their oral tradition, miracles of which no other known people have been capable. Such a faith does not fall within my category of 'rational disagreement'. The only possible rational conclusion from the evidence has been summed up in the subtitle of an important recent book on chronology and oral tradition, 'Quest for a Chimera'.*

In the absence of dated written documents, archaeology, and archaeology alone, gives us a chronological framework. The difficulty faced by Schliemann, his contemporaries and immediate successors, was that they had too much leeway. It is sufficient to consider the 1893 volume of Eduard Meyer's *Geschichte des Altertums*. Meyer had studied all the available archaeological publications, possessed as penetrating a mind as anyone in the field, and had the further advantage of his knowledge of hieroglyphics and cuneiform. Yet the best he could offer, apart from fixing the *floruit* of Mycenaean civilization in the fifteenth century B.C. from Egyptian synchronizations, was a very vague pattern which looked like this: The Stone Age was followed on both sides of the Aegean by a common culture he called 'Trojan', which was replaced on the mainland, in particular by the Mycenaean. The latter was so advanced in technique and 'civilization' that we must allow a long gestation period, starting perhaps about 2000 B.C., and a long declining period until the appearance of what we now call 'geometric pottery'.

Meyer was too disciplined and historically minded to mislead himself into thinking he knew more than his evidence permitted, at least about the Trojan War. He accepted the historical kernel, and no more, and he complained specifically that 'the expedition

* D. F. Henige, *The Chronology of Oral Tradition* (Oxford, 1974).

against Troy cannot be set into a firm historical context'. Others, lacking the qualities I have just mentioned, could not resist the freedom offered by centuries among which to roam and they provided such contexts and combinations as suited their fancy. Today the margin has been reduced drastically, so that few contexts or combinations are any longer available. I need not catalogue all the advances of the past hundred years that have brought about this result. I shall mention merely Furumark's establishment of a chronology of Mycenaean pottery, not merely because it was perhaps the most important single contribution in the struggle for a chronology but also because it best exemplifies the difficulties today.

Even archaeologists have constantly to be reminded, though they of course know it, that a pottery chronology such as Furumark's is not the equivalent of a chronology of the kings of England. What Caskey said of the date of the destruction of Troy VIIa, that we 'must allow a latitude of some twenty or thirty years toward the end of the thirteenth century', applies to every other archaeologically based date. Professionals appreciate that when they see such dates as c. 1260 scattered throughout an archaeological publication; the layman does not, and it is astonishing how often the professionals proceed to forget it themselves. They forget it because it is an intolerable obstacle: a latitude of twenty or thirty years is too wide when one is seeking a historical context for a war, in our case for the Trojan War. But it is too narrow for the freedom to roam which Schliemann and his immediate successors enjoyed, and that is why I spoke of the paradox of increasing knowledge.

We find ourselves in this predicament because Homer provides no context. Homer's war, the war of the poems and of the tradition, is a timeless event floating in a timeless world, and, in the sense in which I have been using the word, in a non-contextual world. The story of Paris and Helen and Menelaus is the proximate cause, like the assassination at Sarajevo in 1914, but it is not a context. Other peers have been assassinated and other noble ladies have been abducted without embroiling half of the world in a great war. What I have been calling a context, after

Eduard Meyer, is the complex social and political situation, in and between the 'nations' involved, which led to war in one or another case, not in others; not to war in general, but to a specific war, waged by specific combatants on a specific scale, and so on.

The archaeology of Troy has added nothing. But the archaeology of mainland Greece, Asia Minor, Cyprus, and Syria, which produced important new documents, offers hitherto unknown or unappreciated possibilities. We know that the end of the thirteenth century saw widespread devastation throughout the Peloponnese and in central Greece, the break-up of the Hittite empire, destruction in Cyprus and in northern Syria. Documents from Cyprus and from Ugarit in northern Syria, tantalizing and fragmentary though they are, leave little room for doubt that some form of massive marauding activity lay behind these almost simultaneous devastations, and more and more experts are coming to link that activity with two Egyptian texts, long known, from which the appellation 'Sea Peoples' is derived. And the temptation grows to place the destruction of Troy VIIa in the same context.

So long as the obdurate silence from and about Troy persists in contemporary documents, that can be no more than an hypothesis. But it is an hypothesis which provides a recognizable and plausible context; one, furthermore which arises from the ground, so to speak, not from the stratosphere, unlike recent suggestions that the Trojan War was an 'unsuccessful attempt to restore a falling empire', or an 'expedition to secure the Hellespont' made necessary because Troy had become an 'untrustworthy guardian'.

All such suggestions, the plausible as well as the implausible, contradict substantially the Homeric picture of the Trojan War, and that brings me to a methodological principle. Before stating it, I must stop to stress that it is not only archaeology which has advanced enormously since Schliemann's day. Our understanding of oral traditions, and of heroic poetry as a form of oral tradition, has advanced equally, and I am unable to understand why this new knowledge does not receive the same welcome as the archaeological (when its existence is noticed at all, which is not always the case). To argue against the comparative evidence, with Caskey, that ' "faith" in the value of early Greek tradition is a quite respectable possession', is to abandon historical inquiry for a quasi-theological concept. Without faith, for which no foundation is offered or can be offered, reason suggests that when Homer (or any other oral tradition) conflicts directly with written documents (in our case the Linear B tablets) or archaeological finds, with respect to the past which Homer appears to be, and no doubt believed himself to be, narrating, Homer must be abandoned.

That is my methodological principle, and I shall briefly illustrate how little remains of Homer today as a witness for the world in which the Trojan War is traditionally held to have occurred, at those points for which either of the two kinds of evidence I have just mentioned is available. It would almost be enough to compare the relatively lengthy and optimistic list of Homeric-Mycenaean parallels in the material remains to be found in Helen Lorimer's *Homer and the Monuments*, published in 1950, with the paltry half-dozen or so that survived by the time Kirk's *Songs of Homer* appeared in 1962. Since then, the Homeric palace and the Homeric war-chariot have been jettisoned, together with their accoutrements. And, finally, the worst blow of all: the surrender of the last bastion, Homer's 'Mycenaen geography'. Chadwick has recently summed up his conclusions on this subject: 'I believe the Homeric evidence to be almost worthless. . . . One major reason is precisely the complete lack of contact between Mycenaean geography as now known from the tablets and from archaeology on the one hand, and from Homeric accounts on the other. The attempts which have been made to reconcile them, as on p. 143 [of the first edition], are unconvincing.'*

This collapse of Homer on the witness-stand, it will surely have been noticed, is restricted to material objects, and the cross-examination was based on the discoveries not at Troy but at a

* M. Ventris and J. Chadwick, *Documents in Mycenaean Greek* (2nd ed., Cambridge, 1973), p. 415.

host of places in Greece and elsewhere, other than Troy. We are then left with large areas of human behaviour in which either archaeology or contemporary documents, or both, fail to offer any controls for the Homeric tales, at least in the present state of knowledge; areas, furthermore, in which archaeology alone, without documents, is never likely to do so. How are we to judge our ancient witness when there is no common ground, when the other types of evidence neither conflict nor contradict nor corroborate? The range of topics to which that question applies runs the gamut from religion and sexual relations to the Trojan War itself, the one topic with which I have been concerning myself. Neither the war nor Troy itself is mentioned in any contemporary document in any language, from any excavation, so far as I know. The question thus narrows to archaeology and the Homeric Trojan War.

Schliemann, we remember, began his archaeological career by digging for the palace of Odysseus, the hut of Eumaeus, and so on, and he was promptly rebuked: 'a little more criticism might have saved him a good deal of trouble'. He then moved on to Troy, seeking Priam's palace and Hector's grave and the camp of the Achaean besiegers. But this time, not only was he not rebuked, he was followed with growing enthusiasm by a century of archaeological efforts and claims. Yet, I submit, the questions he posed at Troy were as unreal as those he had posed in Ithaca, unreal in the sense that archaeology cannot be expected to produce answers (unless it turns up documents). What we call the Trojan War was, after all, only a single siege supposed to have occurred more than 3000 years ago, of a fortified city that remained in continuous occupation for at least another 1500 years thereafter, during which there were two massive earth-moving operations apart from the normal year-by-year constructions and demolitions. How is it imagined that archaeology can confirm the following matters of fact, which I repeat once again from Blegen's statements of what he believes the excavations to have confirmed (accepting for the sake of the argument that Hissarlik is Homer's Troy): (1) Troy was destroyed by a war; (2) the destroyers were a coalition from the mainland of Greece;

(3) the leader of the coalition was a king named Agamemnon; (4) Agamemnon's overlordship was recognized by the other chieftains; (5) Troy, too, headed a coalition of allies?

The only answer I am able to discover to my question in all the outpouring on the subject is that archaeological discoveries have not contradicted Homer on those five points. But that is not an answer, it merely stands the question on its head. If archaeology cannot confirm such 'facts', it cannot, for the same reason, falsify them (unless it produces some such extreme evidence as that mainland Greece was unoccupied at the time, or similar improbabilities). The Trojan War is not unique in this respect. No one turns to the spade to test the account of Attila in the *Nibelungenlied* or the South Slav epic version of the battle of Kossovo, not merely because it is unnecessary to do that, given the availability of documentation, but also because it would be an acknowledged waste of time. The fact that we have no documentation for the Trojan War does not alter the limits of archaeology in the slightest, it merely injects a large element of melancholy into the situation, and of desperation. There is at present a strong current among non-classical archaeologists to divorce themselves from what they have called 'counterfeit history' in one or another, equally pejorative, synonym. Schliemann's Troy unfortunately provides them with powerful ammunition.

Even Schliemann conceded distortions and fictions in the Homeric tale. What are the stigmata, I ask (not for the first time), which expose a distortion, an anachronism, or an outright fiction so as to distinguish it from a supposed 'reminiscence' of historical fact? In 1878, Charles Newton, Keeper of Greek and Roman Antiquities in the British Museum, reviewing Schliemann's book on Mycenae at great length for the *Edinburgh Review*, wrote: 'How much of the story of Agamemnon is really to be accepted as fact, and by what test we may discriminate between that which is merely plausible fiction and that residuum of true history which can be detected under a mythic disguise in this and other Greek legends, are problems as yet unsolved, notwithstanding the immense amount of erudition and subtle criticism which has been expended on them.' Almost a century has gone by since Newton wrote that, and his conclusion remains the least sceptical one we have a right, on the evidence, to hold today. Some of us are more sceptical: Homer's Trojan War, we suggest, must be evicted from the *history* of the Greek Bronze Age.

BIBLIOGRAPHICAL ESSAY*

INTRODUCTION

Year after year Homer is the subject of a staggering number of publications in all Western languages, and a few in the East as well. For an account of the main trends in the past two centuries, see J. L. Myres, *Homer and His Critics*, ed. Dorothea Gray (London: Routledge & Kegan Paul, 1958); of the most recent developments, A. Heubeck, *Die homerische Frage* (Darmstadt: Wissenschaftliche Buchgesellschaft, 1974); A. Lesky, *Homeros*, reprinted from *Paulys Realencyclopädie der classischen Altertumswissenschaft*, Supplement-Band XI (Stuttgart: Alfred Druckenmüller, 1967). The year-by-year publications are recorded in *L'Année philologique*.

The aim of the following pages is to suggest a small number of works in which the reader will find more extensive discussions of various points raised in this book as well as alternative interpretations. The emphasis is on the more recent publications, most of which have bibliographies of the older literature. When possible, preference has been given to books and articles in English, and, among those, to works which, though written by scholars, require neither knowledge of Greek on the part of the reader nor expert acquaintance with Greek history.

M. Cary, *The Geographic Background of Greek and Roman History* (Oxford, 1949), and G. S. Kirk, *The Nature of Greek Myths* (Penguin, 1974), provide excellent introductions to their respective subjects. On the more theoretical problems in the study of myths, see also Kirk, *Myth* (California and Cambridge, 1970); P. S.

---

* Place of publication is not given for Penguin books, serials or university press publications. The latter are cited in short form: thus, Chicago = University of Chicago Press; Oxford = both Oxford University Press and Clarendon Press.

Cohen, 'Theories of Myth', in *Man*, 4 (1969), pp. 337-53. On the early Greek communities of Asia Minor, in which the Homeric poems were composed, see J. M. Cook, *The Greeks in Ionia and the East* (New York: Praeger; London: Thames & Hudson, 1963), chap. 1-2. The most recent views on the evolution of the Greek language are analysed by J. Chadwick, 'The Prehistory of the Greek Language', in *Cambridge Ancient History*, 3rd ed., vol. 2, pt. 2 (Cambridge, 1975), chap. 39(a).

For a critical discussion of the methodological problems and difficulties inherent in any attempt to employ Greek myths and oral traditions and the Homeric poems in a historical reconstruction, I may refer to three of my essays: 'Myth, Memory and History', in my *The Use and Abuse of History* (New York: Viking; London: Chatto & Windus, 1975), chap. 1, and the two reprinted in this volume as Appendices; and to Franz Hampl, 'Die "Ilias" ist kein Geschichtsbuch', in his *Geschichte als kritische Wissenschaft*, vol. 2 (Darmstadt: Wissenschaftliche Buchgesellschaft, 1975), pp. 51-99. What may be called the 'Mycenaean view' of the world of Odysseus, rejected in the present volume, dominates *A Companion to Homer*, ed. A. J. B. Wace and F. H. Stubbings (New York and London: Macmillan, 1962), on which see P. Vidal-Naquet, 'Homère et le monde mycénien, à propos d'un livre récent et d'une polémique ancienne', in *Annales: Economies, Sociétés, Civilisations*, 18 (1963), pp. 703-19.

HOMER AND ORAL POETRY

C. M. Bowra, *Heroic Poetry* (New York and London. Macmillan, 1952), is the most comprehensive study of heroic poetry as a *genre*, with rich illustrative material from all over the world. Further insights will be found in his *The Meaning of a Heroic Age*, a 1957 lecture reprinted in *The Language and Background of Homer*, ed. G. S. Kirk (Cambridge, Eng.: Heffer, 1964), chap. 2. Kirk's *The Songs of Homer* (Cambridge, 1962) remains much the best introduction to the problems, historical, linguistic and literary, raised by the Homeric poems. A shortened paperback version is available under the title, *Homer and the Epic* (Cambridge, 1965).

The formulas and other technical aspects of the Homeric poems must be studied technically (and this section of the bibliography will therefore not be of much use to a Greekless reader). The papers of Milman Parry, which underlie all recent analysis, have been collected under the title, *The Making of Homeric Verse*, edited with a lengthy and important introduction by Adam Parry (Oxford, 1971). On the contemporary bards of Yugoslavia, from whom Parry gained much insight, see A. B. Lord, *The Singer of Tales* (Harvard, 1960), a book which is accessible to the non-specialist.

Of more recent publications, I single out the following which have contributed most to the views I have adopted: A Hoekstra, *Homeric Modifications of Formulaic Prototypes*, published in the *Verhandelingen* of the Dutch Academy, n.s. vol. 71, no. 1 (1965); Adam Parry, 'Have we Homer's "Iliad"?' in *Yale Classical Studies*, 20 (1966), pp. 177-216; J. B. Hainsworth, *The Flexibility of the Homeric Formula* (Oxford, 1968); Bernard Fenik, *Typical Battle Scenes in the Iliad* (*Hermes*, Einzelschrift 21, 1968), and *Studies in the Odyssey* (*Hermes*, Einzelschrift 30, 1974); A. Dihle, *Homer-Probleme* (Opladen: Westdeutscher Verlag, 1970). The most powerful defender of the thesis that the *Iliad* and *Odyssey* were composed orally is G. S. Kirk, whose relevent essays are collected in his *Homer and the Oral Tradition* (Cambridge, 1976). An attractive, but untestable, 'Chomskyan' hypothesis about the formulaic procedure has been put forth by M. N. Nagler, 'Towards a Generative View of the Oral Formula', in *Transactions of the American Philological Association*, 98 (1967), pp. 269-311, later incorporated, not always for the better, in his *Spontaneity and Tradition: A Study in the Oral Art of Homer* (California, 1974).

HOMER, THE TROJAN WAR, AND ARCHAEOLOGY

Every history of Greece attempts to place the world of the Homeric poems (as well as the Trojan War) in its relationship with both the older civilizations of the Aegean and with the later history of the Hellenes. For a brief introduction, see my *Early Greece: The Bronze and Archaic Ages* (New York: Norton; London:

Chatto & Windus, 1970); for a detailed account of the period 1100-650 B.C., C. G. Starr, *The Origins of Greek Civilization* (New York: Knopf, 1961; London: Cape, 1962).

The best survey of the Bronze Age archaeology is provided by Emily Vermeule, *Greece in the Bronze Age* (Chicago, 1964), written from the point of view that 'Homer has been rejected as evidence'; of the 'Dark Age', by A. M. Snodgrass, *The Dark Age of Greece* (Edinburgh, 1971), who is sceptical of the historicity of Homeric society. See also Sinclair Hood, *The Minoans* (New York: Praeger; London: Thames & Hudson, 1974); R. W. Hutchinson, *Prehistoric Crete* (Penguin, 1962); J. T. Hooker, *Mycenaen Greece* (Boston and London: Routledge & Kegan Paul, 1976); Lord William Taylour, *The Mycenaeans* (New York: Praeger; London: Thames & Hudson, 1964); C. W. Blegen, *Troy and the Trojans* (New York: Praeger; London: Thames & Hudson, 1963). A popular account of Aegean archaeology will be found in Paul MacKendrick, *The Greek Stones Speak* (New York: St Martin's Press; London: Methuen, 1965).

The series, in German, called *Archaeologia Homerica*, ed. F. Matz and H.-G. Buchholz (Göttingen: Vandenhoeck & Rupprecht), which is still in progress, not only varies greatly in quality but also shows wide disagreement among the individual authors as to which archaeological period is 'Homeric'. The fascicle by Heinrich Drerup, with the unambiguous title, *Griechische Baukunst in geometrischer Zeit* (vol. II, ch. O, 1969), is decisive in linking Homeric building descriptions, in so far as they are not poetic fancy, to the post-Mycenaean centuries; cf. more generally Jan Bouzek, *Homerisches Griechenland* (*Acta Univ. Carolina*, vol. 29, Prague, 1969).

The basic work on the Linear B tablets remains Michael Ventris and John Chadwick, *Documents in Mycenaean Greece*, but it is essential to use the 2nd edition (Cambridge, 1973), with its extensive corrections, additions and re-interpretations by Chadwick. In 'Homer and Mycenae: Property and Tenure', in *Historia*, 6 (1967), pp. 133-59, reprinted in *The Language and Background of Homer* already mentioned, I demonstrated that a sharp break exists in the language of property and social status between the tablets and the Homeric poems. The standard account of the decipherment of the tablets is that of John Chadwick, *The Decipherment of Linear B* (2nd ed., Cambridge, 1968).

The most serious effort to find documentary support in Hittite texts for the traditional account of the Trojan War was made by D. L. Page, *History and the Homeric Iliad* (California, 1959). More precisely, he argued that the Hittite documents provided background, since neither the war nor Troy is mentioned, and the key to his argument was the (controversial) identification of the Achchiyava of the documents with the Achaeans of Homer. That identification now seems to me refuted: see Gerd Steiner, 'Die Ahhijawa-Frage heute', in *Saeculum*, 15 (1964), pp. 365-92; J. D. Muhly, 'Hittites and Achaeans: Ahhijawa *Redomitus*', in *Historia*, 23 (1974), pp. 129-45. Another study by Muhly, 'Homer and the Phoenicians', in *Berytus*, 19 (1970), pp. 19-64, bears on the discussion.

The fundamental arguments in the controversy over the historicity of Homer's Trojan War are marshalled in my 'The Trojan War', with replies by J. L. Caskey, G. S. Kirk and D. L. Page, in *Journal of Hellenic Studies*, 84 (1964), pp. 1-20.

INSTITUTIONS

Of the most important recent institutional analyses, three seem to me to be excessively confident of our ability to penetrate the details of the Linear B tablets: Alfonso Mele, *Società e lavoro nei poemi omerici*, published by the Istituto di Storia e Antichità Greche e Romane of the Univ. of Naples (1968); Ja. A. Lencman, *Die Sklaverei im mykenischen und homerischen Griechenland*, transl. from the Russian by Maria Bräuer-Pospelova (Wiesbaden: Steiner, 1966); Sigrid Deger, *Herrschaftsformen bei Homer* (diss. Vienna: Notring, 1970). The fourth, P. A. L. Greenhalgh, *Early Greek Warfare* (Cambridge, 1973), argues convincingly for a sharp break from Mycenaean practices.

On the political structure, Rolan Martin, *Recherches sur l'agora grecque* (*Bibliothèque des Écoles françaises d'Athènes et de Rome*, vol. 174, 1951), remains valuable. On the *oikos* and the family, see W. K. Lacey, *The Family in Classical Greece* (Cornell; London:

Thames & Hudson, 1968), chap. 2; my 'Marriage, Sale and Gift in the Homeric World', in *Revue international des droits de l'antiquité*, 3rd ser., 2 (1955), pp. 167-94, with a possible modification, regarding Penelope, suggested by Lacey, 'Homeric *hedna* and Penelope's *kyrios*', in *Journal of Hellenic Studies*, 86 (1966), pp. 55-69. The fullest introduction in English to the old view of a linear evolution from clan to state, which ignores the significance of the *oikos*, will be found in Gustave Glotz, *The Greek City and Its Institutions*, transl. N. Mallinson (New York: Knopf; London: Kegan Paul, 1929), pp. 1-60. What might be called a midway position is the lengthy account of Homeric 'chivalry' in H. Jeanmaire, *Couroi et Courètes* (*Travaux et Mémoires de l'Université de Lille*, no. 21, 1939; reprint, New York: Arno, 1975), chap. 1. On labour, technology and the attitudes to them among the archaic Greeks, see also J.-P. Vernant, *Mythe et pensée chez les Grecs* (Paris: Maspero, 1965), chap. 4 (an English translation by Janet Lloyd is forthcoming); on the institutionalized ritual of supplication, J. P. Gould, '*Hiketeia*', in *Journal of Hellenic Studies*, 93 (1973), pp. 74-103; on archaic gift-giving generally, though strangely without reference to the Greeks, Marcel Mauss, *The Gift*, transl. Ian Cunnison (Illinois: Free Press, 1954; London: Cohen & West, 1954).

The position of the Phaeacians between legend and reality is brought out by C. P. Segal, 'The Phaeacians and the Symbolism of Odysseus', in *Arion*, 1 (1962), no. 4, pp. 17-64; and in the final pages of P. Vidal-Naquet, 'Valeurs religieuses et mythiques de la terre et des sacrifices dans l'Odyssée', in *Problèmes de la terre en Grèce ancienne*, ed. M. I. Finley (Paris and the Hague: Mouton, 1973), pp. 269-92.

MORALS AND VALUES

In the first edition of this book, I wrote: 'There could be no better way to begin a study of the Homeric image of man and his gods than by reading in two recent complementary books: Bruno Snell, *The Discovery of the Mind*, transl. T. G. Rosenmeyer (New York: Harper & Row; Oxford, Blackwell, 1953), especially chap. 1, 2, 8; and E. R. Dodds, *The Greeks and the Irrational* (California,

1951), chap. 1-3.' That is still a valid statement, though I might well have added the considerably older book of Gilbert Murray, now out of fashion, *The Rise of the Greek Epic* (3rd ed., Oxford, 1924), which is full of insights despite its antedated conception of the composition of the Homeric poems.

Of recent books, two seem to me outstanding: A. W. H. Adkins, *Merit and Responsibility* (Oxford, 1960), chap. 1-3; and the long, subtle and complex *Nature and Culture in the Iliad: The Tragedy of Hector*, by J. M. Redfield (Chicago, 1975). Atkins has elaborated his analysis in a series of articles, of which I mention 'Homeric Values and Homeric Society' and 'Homeric Gods and the Values of Homeric Society', in *Journal of Hellenic Studies*, 91 (1971), pp. 1-14, and 92 (1972), pp. 1-19, respectively. The former is a reply to a sharp but on the whole not persuasive critique by A. A. Long, 'Morals and Values in Homer', in the same journal, 90 (1970), pp. 121-39.

On special topics, see E. Ehnmark, *The Idea of God in Homer* (Uppsala: Almqvist & Wiksell, 1935), dealing with the concept of divinity as distinct from myths about the individual gods; R. K. Yerkes, *Sacrifice in Greek and Roman Religions and Early Judaism* (New York: Scribner's, 1952; London, Black, 1953), which stresses the element of joyful sharing; G. S. Kirk, 'War and the Warrior in the Homeric Poems', in *Problèmes de la guerre en Grèce ancienne*, ed. J.-P. Vernant (Paris and The Hague: Mouton, 1968) pp. 93-117; N. Himmelmann, *Ueber bildende Kunst in der homerischen Gesellschaft* (*Abhandlungen der geistes- und sozialwissenschaftlichen Klasse, Akademie der Wissenschaften und der Literatur*, Mainz, 1969, no. 7), a more wide-ranging study than the title indicates, neatly complemented by Felix Eckstein, *Handwerk* I, in *Archaeologia Homerica*, already mentioned, vol. 2, chap. L (1974).

EPILOGUE

The subject of W. J. Verdenius, *Homer, the Educator of the Greeks*, published in the *Mededelingen* of the Dutch Academy, n.s. vol.33, no. 5 (1970), is evident from the title. The essential background is provided by Sir Frederic Kenyon, *Books and Readers in Ancient*

Greece and Rome (2nd ed., Oxford, 1951); and H. I. Marrou, *A History of Education in Antiquity*, transl. G. Lamb (New York: New American Library, 1964; London: Sheed & Ward, 1956; an unreliable translation of a work now in its 6th ed. in the original). An account of ancient Greek scholarship on Homer will be found in R. Pfeiffer, *History of Classical Scholarship* (Oxford, 1968); of the debate between Christians and pagans over Homer, in Jean Pepin, *Mythe et allégorie. Les origines grecques et les contestations judéo-chrétiennes* (Paris: Aubier, 1958), pp. 86-214.

In *The Ulysses Theme* (rev. ed., Michigan; Oxford: Blackwell, 1963), W. B. Stanford examines the remarkably varied images of Odysseus from antiquity to our own day. On Homeric themes in early Greek art, see K. Friis Johansen, *The Iliad in Early Geeek Art* (Copenhagen: Munksgaard, 1967); Karl Schefold, *Myth and Legend in Early Greek Art*, transl. Audrey Hicks (New York: Abrams; 1966). M. B. Scherer, *The Legends of Troy in Art and Literature* (New York and London: Phaidon, 1963), ranges through the centuries; though the nearly 200 pictures are most attractive, the reproductions are often too small in scale and the text is not professional enough.

INDEX OF PASSAGES QUOTED

NOTE: *All the translations quoted in the text are the author's, except the quotations from Hesiod and the* Hymn to Apollo. *Italic figures indicate pages in this book.*

GENERAL INDEX

GENERAL INDEX